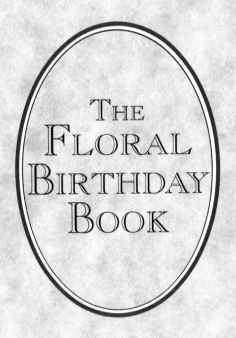

THE
FLORAL
BIRTHDAY
BOOK

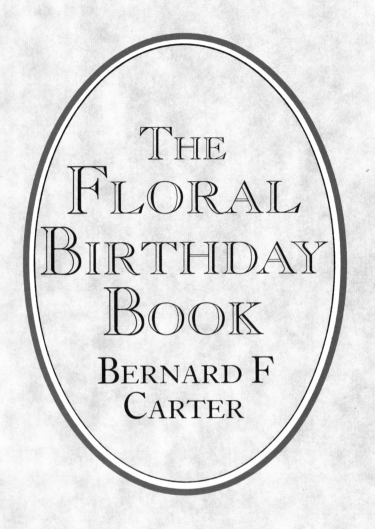

THE FLORAL BIRTHDAY BOOK

BERNARD F CARTER

Bloomsbury Books
London

For
my wife
Irene

First published in Great Britain 1990 by
Webb & Bower (Publishers) Limited
5 Cathedral Close, Exeter, Devon EX1 1EZ

Designed by Vic Giolitto

This edition published by Bloomsbury Books, an imprint of
The Godfrey Cave Group Limited, 42 Bloomsbury Street, London, WC1B 3QJ,
under licence from Webb & Bower Ltd

ISBN 1 85471 059 1

Printed and bound in Great Britain by
BPCC Hazells Ltd
Member of BPCC Ltd

INTRODUCTION

If it is at all possible to have the best of both worlds, then I must surely have come very close to it. From my mother I inherited a talent which later developed into a passion for painting, while my father bestowed upon me a great love and respect for books and the written word. It is a fusion of these deep-rooted traits that have resulted in the *Floral Birthday Book*.

The original framework for this book is a Victorian floral birthday book, discovered abandoned in an empty house, its decaying pages held loosely together by a covering of age-old cobwebs. It was to be some years before I realized its true potential, but in the meantime I had the forethought to have it cleverly restored by a book conservator in Frankfurt. It was becoming increasingly handled by clients who were commissioning me to paint for them the flower for their particular day from this book. It was, therefore, a fairly logical step to re-create and interpret the book in my own way, in my own style of watercolour.

Predictably the problems began almost immediately, along with the mammoth task of amassing all the varied specimens required for 366 days of the year, and for the twelve monthly floral composites thrown in for good measure.

I returned to my studio with a ten-month deadline and so the race was on, no garden was now safe from my clutches as I persuaded, harassed and pestered everyone I came into contact with for specimens. Unsuspecting persons were instantly cross-examined on what they may or may not have growing in their garden. The specimens began arriving in bags, in tubes and in plant pots until the studio took on the appearance of a fruit and flower shop. A dozen bags of tree samples arrived from London, collected by an enthusiastic friend who had raided gardens and precariously balanced herself on park railings in order to comply with my requests. A four-foot length of maize came special delivery, while other friends captured a trio of truffles in France. My wife searched the shops in Penzance for pineapples, olives, pomegranates and limes while I snatched the mistletoe and walnuts from a Christmas party and a carnation from the buttonhole of a surprised wedding guest!

Sometimes my working environment would be filled with the heady, exotic scents of jasmines, wallflowers and roses, which lingered on for days. The most notable exception to these being the red valerian whose nauseous aroma guaranteed it a swift eviction from the studio almost before the paint had dried.

A continuous supply of specially fine watercolour brushes with an approximate working life of four days was sent from Frankfurt. Occasionally paranoia would develop when I was reduced to the last few hairs of the last brush when either an erratic post or an unpredictable customs officer delayed their arrival.

The days were long, starting at 9.00 am until perhaps 11.00 pm, virtually every day of every week throughout those ten months, never losing the love of my work, being daunted only once at one stage of this marathon when my strained eyes refused to focus for more than a couple of minutes at a time. This problem finally righted itself, but it slowed down the output considerably for some weeks.

As the period stretched over the winter months it became apparent that many flowers would not be available when I would need them, despite the fact that this last piece of west Cornwall is blessed with a second season for many species. A solution was suggested and worked to a degree and so it came into being that alongside the frozen beans, peas and last summer's blackberries in the chest freezer appeared trays of summer blooms, waiting to be brought briefly back to life in the studio when their time came.

Identification of some of the specimens proved difficult, for in the original book there is a subtle repetition of some plants, the most memorable one requiring some lateral thinking in interpreting American ivy as Virginia creeper, which already appears earlier on in the book. Ilex was another puzzle, I assumed it to be holly *(Ilex aquifolium)* but in fact, somewhat obscurely, it turned out to be holm oak *(Quercus ilex)*. This rather dyslexic labelling, coupled with the obvious fact that some of the flowers appear out of season, is something for which the Victorians are answerable and will therefore, remain a mystery.

On 11 May 1989, I handed over to the publishers all the paintings and, what had been for me, a complete way of life. To part with all this work into which, over those many months, I had intricately painted my thoughts and my feelings left me with a confused sense of sadness and excitement. I was returning home empty-handed with only the little green birthday book that had suddenly become my world. It was all over, but a deeper, inner feeling hoped that perhaps it was just the beginning.

Bernard F Carter
Studio Chycoll
Sancreed
Penzance

JANUARY

Snowdrops

January 1

Lives of great men all remind us,
    We can make our lives sublime,
And, departing, leave behind us
    Footprints on the sands of Time;–

Footprints, that perchance another,
    Sailing o'er Life's solemn main,
A forlorn and shipwrecked brother,
    Seeing, may take heart again.
                    Longfellow

Grass – **UTILITY**

January 2

AH! think, when a hero is sighing,
    What danger in such an adorer!
What woman could think of denying
    The hand that lays laurels before her?

No heart is so guarded around,
    But the smile of a victor would take it;
No bosom could slumber so sound,
    But the trumpet of glory will wake it!
                    Moore

Bay – **GLORY**

January 3

SOME I remember, and will ne'er forget,
My early friends, friends of my evil day,
Friends of my mirth, friends of my misery too;
Friends given by God, in mercy and in love;
My counsellors, my comforters, and guides;
My joy in grief, my second bliss in joy;
Companions of my young desire; in doubt,
My oracles, my wings in high pursuit.
                    Pollock

Ivy – **FRIENDSHIP**

JANUARY 4

He who ascends to mountain tops shall find
The loftiest peaks most wrapt in clouds and
    snow;
He who surpasses, or subdues, mankind,
Must look down on the hate of those below.

Byron

Laurel – **AMBITION**

JANUARY 5

Oh! lady, twine no wreath for me,
Or twine it of the cypress tree!
Too lightly grow the lilies light,
The varnish'd holly's all too bright;
The May-flower and the eglantine
May shade a brow less sad than mine;
But, lady, twine no wreath for me,
Or weave it of the cypress tree.

Scott

Cypress – **MOURNING**

JANUARY 6

But when he came, though pale and wan,
    He looked so great and high,
So noble was his manly front,
    So calm his steadfast eye;
The rabble rout forbore to shout,
    And each man held his breath,
For well they knew the hero's soul
Was face to face with death.

Aytoun

Box – **FIRMNESS**

JANUARY 7

LADY, you are the cruellist she alive,
If you will lead these graces to the
    grave,
And leave the world no copy.
Shakespeare

Ice Plant – **REJECTED ADDRESSES**

JANUARY 8

'Oh! never,' she cried, 'could I think of enshrining
An image whose looks are so joyless and dim;
But yon little god upon roses reclining,
We'll make, if you please, sir, a Friendship of
    him.'
So the bargain was struck; with the little god
    laden,
She joyfully flew to her shrine in the grove:
'Fairwell,' said the sculptor; 'you're not the
    first maiden
Who came but for Friendship, and took away
    Love.'
Moore

Arbutus – **LOVE OR FRIENDSHIP**

JANUARY 9

BLEST Charity! the grace long-suffering, kind,
Which envies not, has no self-vaunting mind;
Is not puffed up, makes no unseemly show,
Seeks not her own, to provocation slow;
No evil thinks, in no unrighteous choice
Takes pleasure, doth in truth rejoice;
Hides all things, still believes, and hopes the
    best,
All things endures, averse to all contest.
Bishop Ken

Turnip – **CHARITY**

JANUARY 10

To climb the trackless mountain all unseen,
With the wild flock, that never needs a fold;
Alone, o'er steeps and foaming falls to lean,–
This is not solitude; 'tis but to hold
Converse with Nature's charms, and view
   her stores unrolled.

Byron

Heath – **SOLITUDE**

JANUARY 11

AND still his name sounds stirring
   Unto the men of Rome,
As the trumpet blast that cries to them
   To charge the Volcean home;
And wives still pray to Juno
   For boys with hearts as bold
As his, who kept the bridge so well,
   In the brave days of old.

Macaulay

Cresses – **STABILITY**

JANUARY 12

OH, haste! hark the shepherd
   Hath waken'd his pipe,
And led out his lambs
   Where the blae-berry's ripe:
The bright sun is tasting
   The dew on the thyme;
Yon glad maiden's lilting
   An old bridal-rhyme.
There's joy in the heaven,
   And gladness on earth –
So come to the sunshine,
   And mix in the mirth.

Allan Cunningham

Houseleek – **VIVACITY**

JANUARY 13

THE angry word suppress'd, the taunting thought;
Subduing and subdued the petty strife
Which clouds the colour of domestic life;
The sober comfort, all the peace which springs,
From the large aggregate of little things,–
On these small cares of daughter, wife, or friend,
The almost sacred joys of home depend.
Hannah More

Sage – **DOMESTIC VIRTUES**

JANUARY 14

STRANGERS yet!
Oh! the bitter thought to scan
All the loneliness of man!–
Nature, by magnetic laws,
Circle into circle draws;
But they only touch when met,
Never mingle – strangers yet!
Lord Houghton

Lichen – **DEJECTION**

JANUARY 15

..... GOD keeps a niche
In heaven to hold our idols; and albeit
He brake them to our faces, and denied
That our close kisses should impair their white,
I know we shall behold them raised, complete,
The dust swept from their beauty,– glorified;
New Memnons singing in the great God-light.
Mrs Barrett Browning

Fir – **ELEVATION**

January 16

AND though I cannot boast, O Health!
　　Of aught besides, but only thee,
I would not change this bliss for wealth,
　　No, not for all the eye can see.

Then hail, sweet charm! ye breezes, blow!
Ransack the flower and blossom'd tree;
All, all your stolen gifts bestow,
　　For Health has granted all to me.

Clare

Iceland Moss – **HEALTH**

January 17

I GIVE thee all, – I can no more
　　Though poor the offering be;
My heart and lute are all the store
　　That I can give to thee.

Moore

Orange – **GENEROSITY**

January 18

BE such, and only such, my friends,
　　Once mine, and mine for ever;
And here's a hand to clasp in theirs,
　　That shall desert them never.

And thou be such, my gentle love,
　　Time, chance, the world defying;
And take – 'tis all I have – a heart
　　That changes but in dying.

Donne

Monterey Cypress – **CONSTANT**

January 19

ABSENT or present, still to thee,
  My friend, what magic spells belong!
As all can tell who share, like me,
  In turn, thy converse and thy song.

But when the dreaded hour shall come,
  By friendship ever deemed too nigh,
And 'Memory,' o'er her Druid's tomb
  Shall weep that aught of thee can die:

How fondly will she then repay
  The homage offered at thy shrine,
And blend, while ages roll away,
  Her name immortally with thine.
                              Byron

Arbor Vitae – **UNCHANGING FRIENDSHIP**

January 20

TOO late for the rose the evening rain –
  Mary Hamilton;
Too late for the lamb the shepherd's pain – Mary
  Hamilton;
Too late at the door the maiden's stroke;
Too late for the plea when the doom hath been spoke!
Too late the balm when the heart is broke –
  Mary Hamilton.
                              Whyte Melville

Laurustinus – **'I DIE IF NEGLECTED'**

January 21

NEVER exceed thy income. Youth may make
Even with the year; but age, if it will hit,
Shoots a bow shot, and lessens still his stake
As the day lessens, and his life with it.
Thy children, kindred, friends, upon thee call:
Before thy journey, fairly part with all.
                              George Herbert

Endive – **FRUGALITY**

JANUARY 22

THROUGH long days of anguish,
　And sad nights, did pain
Forge my shield, Endurance,
　Bright and free from stain.
Adelaide Procter

Ilex – **ENDURANCE**

JANUARY 23

ABOVE the lowly plants it towers,
The fennel, with its yellow flowers;
And in an earlier age than ours,
Was gifted with the wondrous powers,
　Lost vision to restore.

It gave new strength, and fearless mood,
And gladiators fierce and rude
Mingled it in their daily food;
And he who battled and subdued,
　A wreath of fennel wore.
Longfellow

Fennel – **STRENGTH**

JANUARY 24

THE bird that soars on highest wing,
　Builds on the ground her lowly nest;
And she that doth most sweetly sing,
　Sings in the shade when all things rest.
In lark, and nightingale, we see
What honour hath humility.
Montgomery

Ground Ivy – **HUMILITY**

JANUARY 25

OH! star of strength, I see thee stand,
   And smile upon my pain;
Thou beckonest with thy mailèd hand,
   And I am strong again.

The star of the unconquered will,
   He rises in my breast,
Serene, and resolute, and still,
   And calm, and self-possessed.
Longfellow

Cineraria – **A Star**

JANUARY 26

OH, wasteful woman! she who may
   On her sweet self set her own price,
Knowing he cannot choose but pay –
   How has she cheapened Paradise!
How given for nought her priceless gift,
   How spoiled the bread, and spilled the wine,
Which, spent with due respective thrift,
   Had made brutes men, and men divine!
Coventry Patmore

Thyme – **Thriftiness**

JANUARY 27

PEACE be around thee, wherever thou rovest!
   May life be for thee on summer's day;
And all that thou wishes, and all that thou lovest,
Come smiling around thy sunny way.

If sorrow e'er this calm should break,
   May even thy tears pass off so lightly,
Like spring showers, they'll only make
   The smiles that follow shine more brightly.
Moore

Olive – **Peace**

January 28

Now fades the glimmering landscape on the sight,
And all the air a solemn stillness holds,
Save where the beetle wheels her droning flight,
And drowsy tinklings lull the distant folds.

Save that from yonder ivy-mantled tower
The moping owl does to the moon complain,
Of such as, wandering near her secret bower,
Molest her ancient solitary reign.

Gray

Stonecrop – **Tranquillity**

January 29

'Chloris, I swear, by all I ever swore,
That from this hour I shall not love thee more.'
'What! love no more? Oh, why this alter'd vow?'
'Because I *cannot* love thee *more* – than now.'

Moore

Truffle – **Surprise**

January 30

And her against sweet Cheerfulnesse was placed,
Whose eyes, like twinkling stars in evening cleare,
Were deckt with smiles, and all sad humours chased,
And darted forth delight, the which her goodly
    graced.

Spenser

Variegated Holly – **Always Cheerful**

January 31

THE seraph Abdiel, faithful found
Among the faithless, faithful only he;
Among innumerable false, unmoved,
Unshaken, unseduced, unterrified,
His loyalty he kept, his love, his zeal;
Nor number, nor example with him wrought,
To swerve from truth, or change his constant mind.

Milton

White Ivy – **Rarity**

FEBRUARY

Daffodils

Snowdrops (seed heads)

Camellia

Lesser periwinkle

Lesser celandine

February 1

....So we grew together,
Like to a double cherry, seeming parted,
But yet a union in partition;
Two lovely berries moulded on one stem:
So, with two seeming bodies, but one heart;
Two of the first, like coats in heraldry,
Due but to one, and crowned with one crest.
And will you rent our ancient love asunder,
To join with men in scorning your poor friend?

Shakespeare

Corsican Pine – 'YOU BEWILDER ME'

February 2

Has Hope, like the bird in the story
    That flitted from tree to tree,
With the talisman's glittering glory –
    Has Hope been that bird to thee?

On branch after branch alighting,
    The gem did she still display,
And when nearest and most inviting,
    Then waft the fair gem away?

Moore

Snowdrop – HOPE

February 3

'And on!' said the youth, 'since tomorrow I go,
    To fight in a far distant land,
Your tears for my absence soon ceasing to flow,
Some other will court you, and you will bestow,
    On a wealthier suitor your hand.'
'Oh! hush those suspicions!' fair Imogine said,
    'Offensive to love and to me;
For if you be living, or if you be dead,
I swear by the Virgin that none in your stead
    Shall husband of Imogine be!'

Lewis

Champignon – SUSPICION

FEBRUARY 4

ALAS! that Poverty's evil eye
   Should e'er come hither
   Such sweets to wither!
The flowers laid down their heads to die,
And Hope fell sick as the witch drew nigh.
   She came one morning,
   Ere Love had warning,
And raised the latch where the young god lay:
'Oh, oh!' said Love, 'is it you? Goodbye!'
So he opened the window, and flew away.
                  Moore

Clematis – **POVERTY**

FEBRUARY 5

   THEY tell thee to doubt me,
   And think of me no more;
   They say I have sported
   With other hearts before:
But when you hear unkind ones speak,
With venomed tongue and smiling cheek,
   Repel them, and tell them
   That I've been true to thee.
                  Old Song

Crocus – **ABUSE NOT**

FEBRUARY 6

O THOU, the friend of man assign'd,
With balmy hands his wounds to bind,
   And charm his frantic woe;
When first distress, with dagger keen,
Broke forth to waste his destined scene,
   His wild unsated foe!

By Pella's bard, a magic name –
By all the griefs his thought could frame,
   Receive my humble rite:
Long, Pity, let the nation view
Thy sky-worn robes of tenderest blue,
   And eyes of dewy light.
                  Collins

Camellia Japonica – **PITY**

FEBRUARY 7

CURST be the verse, how well soe'er it flow,
That tends to make one worthy man my foe, –
Give virtue scandal, innocence a fear,
Or from the soft-eyed virgin steal a tear.

Pope

Opuntia – **SATIRE**

FEBRUARY 8

BUT 'tis not to list to the waterfall,
That Parisina leaves her hall;
And it is not to gaze on the heavenly light
That the lady walks in the shadow of night.

And if she sits in Este's bower;
'Tis not for the sake of its full-blown flower;
She listens – but not for the nightingale,
Though her ear expects as soft a tale.

Byron

Almond Tree – **INDISCRETION**

FEBRUARY 9

HOW canst thou renounce the boundless store
Of charms which Nature to her votary yields, –
The warbling woodland, the resounding shore,
The pomp of groves, and garniture of fields:
All that the genial ray of morning gilds,
And all that echoes to the song of even;
All that the mountain's sheltering bosom yields,
And all the dread magnificence of Heaven,
Oh, how canst thou renounce, and hope to be
        forgiven?

Beattie

Kalmia – **NATURE**

FEBRUARY 10

LIGHTSOME, brightsome cousin mine,
Easy, breezy Caroline!
With thy locks all raven shaded,
From thy merry brow up-braided,
And thine eyes of laughter full,
  Brightsome cousin mine!
Thou in chains of love hast bound me,
Wherefore dost thou flit around me,
  Laughter-loving Caroline?
Bon Gaultier

Primula – **ANIMATION**

FEBRUARY 11

HASTE thee, nymph, and bring with thee
Jest and youthful jollity,
Quips and cranks, and wanton wiles,
Nods, and becks, and wreathed smiles,
Such as hang on Hebe's cheek,
And love to live in dimple sleek.
Milton

Spring Crocus – **YOUTHFUL GLADNESS**

FEBRUARY 12

AH! were she as pitiful as she is fair,
Or but as mild as she is seeming so,
Then were my hopes greater than my despair,
Then all the world were heaven, nothing woe.

So as she shows, she seems the budding rose,
Yet sweeter far than is an earthly flower;
Sovereign of beauty, like the spray she grows,
Compass'd she is with thorns and cankered flower;
Yet were she willing to be pluck'd and worn,
She would be gathered though she grew on thorn.
Robert Green

Larch – **DECEITFUL CHARMS**

FEBRUARY 13

MARGARET. – He loves me – not – he loves me – not
 – (*as she plucks off the last leaf with eager delight*)
 – he loves me!
Faust. – Yes, my child, deem this language of the
 flower the answer of an oracle – 'He loves thee!'
Goethe

Tree Poppy – **LOVE'S ORACLE**

FEBRUARY 14

OH! there are looks and tones that dart
An instant sunshine through the heart,
As if the soul that minute caught
Some treasure it through life had sought;
As if those very lips and eyes,
Predestined to have all our sighs,
And never be forgot again,
Sparkled and spoke before us then.
So came thy every look and tone,
When first on me they breathed and shone
New, as if brought from other spheres,
Yet welcome as if loved for years.
Moore

Pyrus Japonica – **LOVE AT FIRST SIGHT**

FEBRUARY 15

I THINK of thee! my thoughts do twine and bud
About thee, as wild vines, about a tree,
Put out broad leaves, and soon there's nought to see,
Except the straggling green which hides the wood.
Mrs Barrett Browning

Irish Ivy – **CLINGING AFFECTION**

FEBRUARY 16

OH, how, or by what means may I contrive
To bring the hour that brings thee back more near?
How may I teach my drooping hope to live
Until that blessed time, and thou art here?

I'll tell thee: for thy dear sake I will lay hold
Of all good aims, and consecrate to thee,
In worthy deeds, each moment that is told,
While thou, beloved one, art far from me.
Fanny Kemble

Purple Violet – 'YOU OCCUPY MY THOUGHTS'

FEBRUARY 17

AWAKE, ye sons of Spain! awake! advance!
Lo! Chivalry, your ancient goddess, cries,
But wields not, as of old, her thirsty lance,
Nor shakes her crimson plumage in the skies:
Now on the smoke of blazing bolts she flies,
And speaks in thunder through yon engines' roar:
In every peal she calls – 'Awake! arise!'
Say, is her voice more feeble than of yore,
When her war-song was heard on Andalusia's shore?
Byron

Daffodil – CHIVALRY

FEBRUARY 18

LIFE, believe, is not a dream
   So dark as sages say;
Oft a little morning rain
   Foretells a pleasant day.
Sometimes there are clouds of gloom,
   But these are transient all;
If the shower will make the roses bloom,
   O why lament its fall?
Charlotte Brontë

Daisy – CHEERFULNESS

February 19

SOME minds are temper'd happily, and mix'd
With such ingredients of good sense, and taste
Of what is excellent in man – they thirst
With such a zeal to be what they approve,
That no restraints can circumscribe them more
Than they themselves by choice, for wisdom's
     sake,
Nor can example hurt them.

Cowper

Flowering Currant – **SELF-REVERENCE**

February 20

HE had no breath, no being but in hers;
She was his voice; he did not speak to her,
But trembled on her words; she was his sight,
For his eye followed hers, and saw with hers,
Which coloured all his objects; he had ceased
To live within himself; she was his life,
The ocean to the river of his thoughts,
Which terminated all; upon a tone,
A touch of hers, his blood would ebb and flow,
And his cheek change tempestuously – his heart
Unknowing of its cause of agony.

Byron

Arum Lily – **ARDOUR**

February 21

NOT lightly did I love, nor lightly choose:
Whate'er thou losest, I will also lose;
If bride of death – being first my chosen bride,
I'll await death, lingering by thy side.

Hon Mrs Norton

Gorse – **ENDURING AFFECTION**

FEBRUARY 22

AND ever against eating cares,
Lap me in soft Lydian airs,
Married to immortal verse,
Such as the melting soul may pierce,
In notes, with many a winding bout
Of linked sweetness long drawn out.
With wanton heed, and giddy cunning,
The melting voice through mazes running,
Untwisting all the chains that tie
The hidden soul of harmony.

Milton

Reeds – **MUSIC**

FEBRUARY 23

As the ore must for ever obedient be found,
   By the loadstone attracted along;
So in England you drew all the poets around,
   By the magical force of your song.

Dr Burney

Variegated Laurel – **ATTRACTIVE**

FEBRUARY 24

THERE was but one spell upon my brain,
Upon my pencil, on my strain;
But one face to my colours came;
My chords replied to but one name –
Lorenzo! – all seemed vowed to thee,
To passion, and to misery!

L E L

Escallonia – **'I LIVE FOR THEE'**

FEBRUARY 25

But thou, O Hope! with eyes so fair,
What was thy delighted measure?
Still it whisper'd promised pleasure,
And bade the lovely scenes at distance hail!
Still would her touch the strain prolong;
And from the rocks, the woods, the vale,
She called on Echo still through all the song;
And where her sweetest theme she chose,
A soft responsive voice was heard at every close,
And Hope enchanted smiled, and waved her
    golden hair.

Collins

Cyclamen – **HOPE**

FEBRUARY 26

On she went, and her maiden smile
In safety lighted her round the Green Isle;
And blest for ever is she who relied
Upon Erin's honour and Erin's pride.

Moore

Hepatica – **CONFIDENCE**

FEBRUARY 27

And when, as how often I eagerly listen
To stories thou read'st of the dear olden day,
How delightful to see our eyes mutually glisten,
And feel that affection has sweeten'd the lay.
Yes, love, – and when wandering at even or
    morning,
Through forest or wild, or by waves foaming
    white,
I have fancied new beauties the landscape
    adorning.
Because I have seen thou wast glad in the sight.

Mary Howitt

Garden Daisy – '**I SHARE YOUR SENTIMENTS**'

FEBRUARY 28

HAPPY those early dayes, when I
Shin'd in my angell-infancy!
Before I understood this place,
Appointed for my second race,
Or taught my soul to fancy aught
But a white, celestial thought;
When yet I had not walkt above
A mile or two from my first love,
And looking back, at that short space,
Could see a glimpse of his bright face.

Vaughan

Buttercup – **CHILDHOOD**

....

FEBRUARY 29

THY husband is thy lord, thy life, thy keeper,
Thy head, thy sovereign; one that cares for thee,
And for thy maintenance; commits his body
To painful labour, both by sea and land,
To watch the night in storms, the day in cold,
While thou liest warm at home, secure and safe;
And craves no other tribute at thy hands,
But love, fair looks, and true obedience, –
Too little payment for so great a debt.

Shakespeare

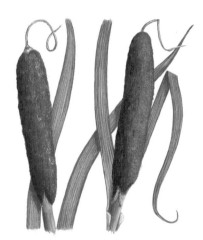

Bullrush – **DOCILITY**

....

MARCH

Three-cornered leek

Narcissus

Blackthorn

Spring crocus

Violet

Primrose

Lesser celandine

March 1

RARELY, rarely comest thou,
　　Spirit of Delight;
Wherefore hast thou left me now,
　　Many a day and night?
Many a weary night and day
'Tis since thou art fled away.

How shall ever one like me
　　Win thee back again?
With the joyous and the free,
　　Thou wilt scoff at pain.
Spirit false! thou hast forgot
All but those who heed thee not.
　　　　　　　　　　Shelley

Willow – **FORSAKEN**

March 2

I AM bound by the old promise;
　　What can break that golden chain?
Not even the words that you have spoken,
　　Or the sharpness of my pain.

Do you think, because you fail me,
　　And draw back your hand to-day,
That from out the heart I gave you,
　　My strong love can fade away?
　　　　　　　　Adelaide Procter

Blue Violet – **FAITHFULNESS**

March 3

OH! how impatience gains upon the soul,
　　When the long-promised hour of joy
　　　　draws near!
How slow the tardy moments seem to roll
　　What spectres rise of inconsistent fear!
To the fond doubting heart its hopes
　　　　appear
　　Too brightly fair, too sweet to realize;
All seem but day-dreams of delight too
　　　　dear!
　　　　　　　　　　Mrs Tighe

Pink Camellia – **ANTICIPATION**

MARCH 4

O WOMAN! in our hours of ease,
Uncertain, coy, and hard to please,
And variable as the shade
By the light quivering aspen made;
When pain and anguish wring the brow,
A ministering angel thou!

Scott

Wallflower – **FIDELITY**

MARCH 5

WI' lightsome heart I pu'd a rose,
 Fu' sweet upon its thorny tree,
And my fause luver stole my rose,
 But, ah! he left the thorn wi' me!

Burns

Garden Anemone – **FORSAKEN**

MARCH 6

SPORT, that wrinkled Care derides,
And Laughter holding both his sides:
Come, and trip it as you go,
On the light fantastic toe.

Milton

Hyacinth – **SPORT**

March 7

.... It's my honest conviction,
That my breast is a chaos of all contradiction:
Religious – deistic – now loyal and warm;
Then a dagger-drawn democrat hot for reform:
This moment a fop – that, sententious as Titus;
Democritus now, and anon Heraclitus:
Now laughing and pleased, like a child with a
      rattle;
Then vexed to the soul with impertinent tattle:
Now moody and sad, now unthinking and gay –
To all points of the compass I veer in a day.
Kirke White

Wild Daisy – **Indecision**

March 8

I'll give thee fairies to attend on thee;
And they shall fetch thee jewels from the deep;
And sing, while thou on pressed flowers dost
      sleep:
And I will purge thy mortal grossness so,
That thou shalt like an airy spirit go.
Shakespeare

Ivy Spray – **Assiduous to please**

March 9

Then why this ceaseless, vain unrest?
Earth opens her impartial breast
To prince and beggar both; nor might
Gold e'er tempt Hell's grim satellite
To waft astute Prometheus o'er
From yonder ghastly Stygian shore.
Proud Tantalus and all his race
He curbs within that rueful place;
The toil-worn wretch, who cries for ease,
Invoked or not, he hears and frees.
Horace

Kingcup – **'I wish I was rich'**

MARCH 10

TRUE modesty is a discerning grace,
And only blushes in the proper place;
But counterfeit is blind, and skulks,
    through fear,
Where 'tis a shame to be ashamed t'ap-
    pear:
Humility the parent of the first,
The last by vanity produced and nursed.
                         Cowper

White Violet – **MODESTY**

MARCH 11

WHO is Sylvia? what is she,
    That all our swains commend her?
Holy, fair, and wise is she,
    The heavens such grace did lend her,
That she might admired be.

Is she kind as she is fair?
    For Beauty lives with kindness;
Love doth to her eyes repair,
    To help him of his blindness;
And being helped, inhabits there.
                       Shakespeare

Marshmallow – **KINDNESS**

MARCH 12

AH! ne'er so dire a thirst of glory boast,
Nor in the critic let the man be lost.
Good nature and good sense must ever join;
To err is human, to forgive Divine.
                         Pope

Cucumber – **CRITICISM**

MARCH 13

STAR-LIKE her eyes – but seem'd suffused with woe,
As thus she spoke, in accents soft and low:
Poet! whose fame shall reach from sea to sea,
Till Heaven's eternal orbs forget to roll,
Oh! haste thee hence, and save a sinking soul,
Forlorn by Fortune, yet beloved by me!

Beatrice sends thee to the world above
(Her bosom throbbing with eternal love,
That leads her from the fount of pure delight),
In mercy to oppose his mad career,
Where yonder paths to swift destruction bear,
She hovers on the bounds of ancient night.

Dante

Double Daffodil – **REGARD**

MARCH 14

THOU sail'st with others in this Argus here,
No wrack or bulging thou hast cause to fear;
But trust to this, my noble passenger:
Who swims with Virtue, he shall still be sure,
Ulysses-like, all tempests to endure,
And 'midst a thousand gulfs to be secure.

Herrick

Mint – **VIRTUE**

MARCH 15

I WOULD I were a careless child,
Still dwelling in my Highland cave,
Or roaming through the dusky wild,
Or bounding o'er the dark blue wave.

Byron

Primrose – **YOUTH**

MARCH 16

WHEN Love is kind,
  Cheerful and free,
Love's sure to find
  Welcome from me;
But when Love brings
  Heartache or pang,
Tears, and such things,
  Love may go hang!
Moore

Mustard – **INDIFFERENCE**

MARCH 17

LADY, where'er you roam, whatever land
Woos the bright touches of that artist hand;
Whether you sketch the valley's golden meads,
Where mazy Linth his lingering current leads;
Enamour'd catch the mellow hues that sleep
At eve on Mielleries' immortal steep:
Or musing o'er the Lake, at day's decline,
Mark the last shadow on that holy shrine,
Where many a night the shade of Tell complains
Of Gullias' triumph, and Helvetia's chains;
Oh! lay the pencil for a moment by,
Turn from the canvas that creative eye,
And let its splendour, like the morning ray
Upon a shepherd's harp, illume my lay.
Moore

Auricula – **PAINTING**

MARCH 18

WE twa ha'run about the braes,
  And pu'd the gowans fine;
But we've wander'd mony a weary foot
  Sin' auld lang syne.
Burns

Red Periwinkle – **EARLY FRIENDSHIPS**

MARCH 19

. . . . A HIDDEN strength,
Which, if Heaven gave it, may be term'd heroism:
'Tis chastity, my brother, chastity:
She that has that, is clad in complete steel,
And, like a quiver'd nymph with arrows keen,
May trace huge forests, and unharbour'd heaths,
Infamous, and sandy perilous wilds.
Where, through the sacred rays of chastity
No savage fierce, bandit, or mountaineer,
Will dare to soil her virgin purity.

Milton

Orange Blossom – **CHASTITY**

MARCH 20

IT is not while beauty and youth are thine own,
    And they cheek unprofaned by a tear,
That the fervour and faith of a soul can be
        known,
    To which time will but make thee more dear.

Moore

Blue Hyacinth – **CONSTANCY**

MARCH 21

DO not trust him, gentle lady,
    Though his voice be low and sweet;
Heed not him who kneels before thee,
    Gently pleading at thy feet.

Coard

Rhubarb – **ADVICE**

March 22

THEY tell me thou'rt the favoured guest
Of every fair and brilliant throng, –
No wit like thine to wake the jest,
No voice like thine to breathe the song.
Moore

Campanula – 'YOU ARE RICH IN ATTRACTION'

March 23

ON her fair cheeks' unfading hue,
The young pomegranate's blossoms strew
Their bloom in blushes ever new;
Her hair in hyacinthine flow,
Then left to roll its folds below,
(As 'midst her handmaids in the hall
She stood superior to them all,)
Hath swept the marble where her feet
Gleamed whiter than the mountain sleet,
Ere from the cloud that gave it birth
It fell, and caught one stain of earth.
Byron

Orchis – A BEAUTY

March 24

YET mark'd I where the bolt of Cupid fell:
It fell upon a little Western flower,
Before milk-white, now purple with Love's wound,
And maidens call it Love in Idleness.
Shakespeare

Wild Violet – LOVE IN IDLENESS

MARCH 25

No one is so accursed by fate,
No one so utterly desolate,
But some heart, though unknown,
Reponds unto his own, –

Responds, as if with unseen wings
An angel touch'd its quivering strings,
And whispers in its song,
Where hast thou stayed so long?
Longfellow

Lenten Lily – **RECIPROCAL LOVE**

MARCH 26

YET once again, but once before we sever,
  Fill we the brimming cup – it is the last;
And let these lips, now parting, and for ever,
  Breathe o'er this pledge the memory of the past!
Mrs Kemble

Double Daisy – **PARTICIPATION**

MARCH 27

THE broken soldier, kindly bade to stay,
Sat by his fire, and talk'd the night away,
Wept o'er his wounds, or, tales of sorrow done,
Shoulder'd his crutch, and show'd how fields were
    won.
Pleased with his guests, the good man learn'd to glow,
And quite forgot their vices in their woe;
Careless their merits or their faults to scan,
His pity gave, ere charity began.
Goldsmith

Peppermint – **CORDIALITY**

MARCH 28

OFT in my waking dreams do I
    Live o'er again that happy hour,
When midway on the mount I lay,
    Beside the ruined tower.

The moonshine stealing o'er the scene,
    Had blended with the light of eve;
And *she* was there, my hope, my joy,
    My own dear Genevieve.

Coleridge

White Periwinkle – **PLEASANT RECOLLECTIONS**

MARCH 29

SAID he – 'I would dream for ever, like the flowing of
    that river,
Flowing ever in a shadow greenly onward to the sea!
So, thou vision of all sweetness, princely to a full
    completeness,
Would my heart and life flow onward, deathward,
    through this dream of *thee.*'

Mrs Barrett Browning

Heartsease – **THOUGHTS**

MARCH 30

SIGH no more, ladies, sigh no more;
    Men were deceivers ever,
One foot on sea, and one on shore,
    To one thing constant never.
    Then sigh not so,
    But let them go,
    And be you blithe and bonny;
Converting all your sounds of woe
    Into, hey nonny, nonny!

Shakespeare

Evening Primrose – **INCONSISTANCY**

March 31

WEALTH, and the high estate of pride,
With what untimely speed they glide,
 How soon depart!
Bid not the shadowy phantoms stay;
The vassals of a mistress they,
 Of fickle heart.

These gifts in Fortune's hands are found;
Her swift revolving wheel turns round,
 And they are gone!
No rest th' inconstant goddess knows,
But changing, and without repose,
 Still hurries on.

Longfellow

Polyanthus – **PRIDE OF RICHES**

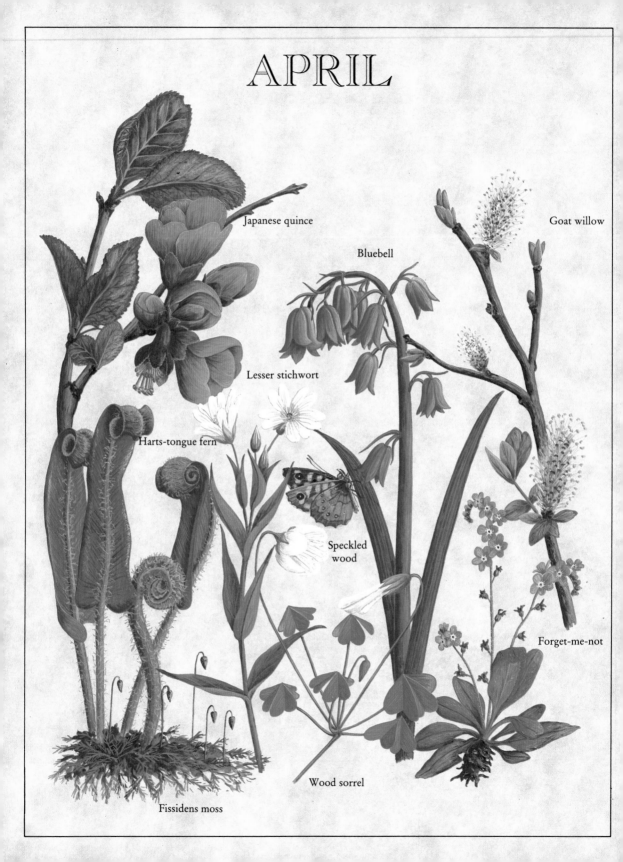

APRIL

Japanese quince

Goat willow

Bluebell

Lesser stichwort

Harts-tongue fern

Speckled wood

Forget-me-not

Wood sorrel

Fissidens moss

April 1

FAREWELL, ye vanishing flowers, that shone
  In my fairy wreath, so bright and brief;
Oh! what are the brightest that e'er have blown,
To the lote-tree springing by Allah's throne,
  Whose flowers have a soul in every leaf?
Joy, joy for ever! my task is done –
The gates are pass'd, and Heaven is won.

Moore

Palm – **VICTORY**

April 2

I, WHO was Fancy's lord, am Fancy's slave,
  Like the low murmurs of the Indian shell,
Ta'en from its coral bed beneath the wave,
  Which, unforgetful of the ocean's swell,
Retains within its mystic urn the hum
  Heard in the sea grots where the Nereids dwell:
Old thoughts still haunt me – unawares they come
  Between me and my rest, nor can I make
Those aged visitors of sorrow dumb.

Aytoun

Purple Hyacinth – **SORROW**

April 3

SUN of the sleepless! melancholy star!
Whose tearful beam shows tremulously far,
That show'st the darkness thou canst not dispel, –
How like art thou to joy remember'd well!
So gleams the past, the light of other days,
Which shines, but warms not, with its powerless rays.
O! nightbeam sorrow watcheth to behold,
Distinct, but distant, clear, but, oh! how cold!

Byron

Cowslip – **PENSIVENESS**

APRIL 4

IF music be the food of love, play on;
Give me excess of it: that surfeiting,
The appetite may sicken, and so die.
Shakespeare

Wood Anemone – **SICKNESS**

APRIL 5

WHAT means this tumult in a Vestal's veins?
Why rove my thoughts beyond this last retreat?
Why feels my heart its long-forgotten heat?
Yet, yet, I love! From Aberlard it came;
An Eloisa yet must kiss the name.
Dear, fatal name! rest ever unreveal'd,
Nor pass these lips in holy silence seal'd:
Hide it, my heart, within that close disguise,
Where, mixed with God's, his loved idea lies.
Pope

Crimson Polyanthus – **THE HEART'S MYSTERY**

APRIL 6

SWEET flower! that with thy soft blue eye,
    Didst once look up in shady spot,
To whisper to the passer-by
    Those tender words, 'Forget-me-not!'

Thou speak'st of hours when I was young,
    And happiness arose unsought;
When she, the whispering woods among,
    Gave me thy bloom, Forget-me-not!
Bon Gaultier

Garden Forget-me-not – **FORGET ME NOT**

April 7

To you my soul's affections move,
　Devoutly, warmly true;
My life has been a task of love,
　One long, long thought of you.

If all your tender faith be o'er,
　If still my truth you'll try,
Alas! I know but one proof more –
　I'll bless your name, and die!
Moore

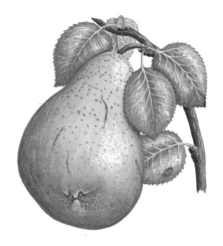

Pear Tree – **Affection**

April 8

And in thy right hand lead with thee
The mountain nymph, sweet Liberty;
And if I give the honour due,
Mirth, admit me of thy crew,
To live with her, and live with thee,
In unreproved pleasures free.
Milton

Saffron Meadow – **Mirth**

April 9

Tell me not, in mournful numbers,
　Life is but an empty dream;
For the soul is dead that slumbers,
　And things are not what they seem.

Life is real! life is earnest!
　And the grave is not its goal;
'Dust thou art, to dust returnest,'
　Was not spoken of the soul.
Longfellow

Lilac Polyanthus – **Confidence in Heaven**

April 10

THY every look, and every grace,
    So charm whene'er I view thee,
Till death o'ertake me in the chase,
    Still will my hopes pursue thee.

Then, when my tedious hours are past,
    Be this last blessing given –
Low at thy feet to breathe my last,
    And die in sight of Heaven!
                    William Hamilton

Globe Ranunculus – 'I AM DAZZLED BY YOUR CHARMS'

April 11

AH me! full sorely is my heart forlorn,
To think how modest worth neglected lies,
While partial Fame doth with her blasts adorn
Such deeds alone as pride and pomp disguise –
Deeds of ill sort, and mischievous emprise.
Lend me thy clarion, goddess! let me try
To sound the praise of merit ere it dies;
Such as I oft have chancèd to espy,
Lost in the shades of dull obscurity.
                    Shenston

Red Primrose – **UNPATRONISED MERIT**

April 12

AND I bend the knee before her,
    As a captive ought to bow:
Pray thee, listen to my pleading,
    Sovereign of my soul art thou!

Oh, my dear and gentle lady,
    Let me show thee all my pain,
Ere the words that late were prisoned
    Sink into my heart again.
                    Aytoun

Peach Blossom – 'I AM YOUR CAPTIVE'

April 13

But if for me thou dost forsake
Some other maid, and rudely break
Her worshipp'd image from its base,
To give to me the ruin'd place;–

Then fare thee well! I'd rather make
My bower upon some icy lake,
When thawing suns begin to shine,
Than trust to love so false as thine!
Moore

Apricot Blossom – **Doubt**

April 14

In everlasting blushes seen,
Such Pringle shines, of sprightly mien;
To her the power of love imparts –
Rich gift! – the soft successful arts
That best the lover's fire provoke, –
The lively step, the mirthful joke,
The speaking glance, the amorous wile,
The sportful laugh, the winning smile.

William Hamilton

Marjoram – **Blushes**

April 15

There is a love that is to last,
When the hot days of youth are past;
Such love did a sweet maid bestow,
One year ago.

I took a leaflet from her braid,
And gave it to another maid:
Love! broken should have been thy bow,
One year ago.
Savage Landor

Wild Ranunculus – **Inconsistancy**

April 16

A LITTLE learning is a dangerous thing;
Drink deep, or taste not the Pierian spring;
There shallow draughts intoxicate the brain,
And drinking largely sobers us again.

Pope

Cherry Tree – **Education**

April 17

'OH, stay! I cried, 'bright vision stay,
 And leave me not forlorn!'
But smiling still they passed away,
 Like shadows of the morn.

One spirit still remained, and cried,
 'Thy soul shall ne'er forget!'
He standeth ever by my side,
 The phantom call'd Regret.

Adelaide Procter

Wistaria – **Regret**

April 18

LESBIA wears a robe of gold,
 But all so close the nymph hath laced it,
Not a charm of Beauty's mould
 Presumes to stay where Nature placed it.
Oh! my Nora's gown for me,
 That floats as wild as mountain breezes,
Leaving every beauty free
 To sink or swell as Heaven pleases.

Moore

Sweetbriar – **Simplicity**

April 19

You smile to see me turn and speak
    With one whose converse you despise;
You do not see the dreams of old
    That with his voice arise;
How can you tell what links have made
      Him sacred in my eyes?

Oh! there are voices of the past,
    Links of a broken chain,
Wings that can bear me back to times
    Which cannot come again;
Yet God forbid that I should lose
    The echoes that remain.
Adelaide Procter

Tendrils of Climbing Plants – **Links**

April 20

So the bells of Memory's wonder city
    Peal for me their old melodious chime;
So my heart pours forth a changeful ditty,
    Sad and pleasant from the bygone time.

Domes and towers and castles, fancy builded,
    There lie lost to daylight's garish beams,
There lie hidden, till unveiled and gilded,
    Glory gilded, by my nightly dreams.
From the German of Muller

Blue Periwinkle – **Pleasures of Memory**

April 21

The clouds are at play in the azure space,
And their shadows at play on the bright green vale;
And here they stretch to the frolic chase,
And there they roll on the easy gale.
There's a dance of leaves in that aspen bower,
There's a titter of winds in that beechen tree,
There's a smile on the fruit, and a smile on the flower,
And a laugh from the brook that runs to the sea.
Bryant

Wood Sorrel – **Joy**

April 22

I TOLD her how he pined; and, ah!
　　The deep, the low, the pleading tone
With which I sang another's love
　　Interpreted my own.

Coleridge

Red Tulip – **Declaration of Love**

April 23

HALF my life is full of sorrow,
　　Half of joy still fresh and new;
One of these lives is a fancy,
　　But the other one is true.

Which, you ask me, is the real life?
　　Which the dream – the joy, or woe?
Hush, friend! it is little matter,
　　And, indeed – I never know.

Adelaide Procter

Shamrock – **Joy in Sorrow**

April 24

As by the shore, at break of day,
A vanquish'd chief expiring ay,
Upon the sands, with broken sword,
He traced his farewell to the free;
And there the last unfinish'd word
He dying wrote, was 'Liberty!'

At night a sea-bird shriek'd the knell
Of him who thus for Freedom fell;
The words he wrote, ere evening came,
Were covered by the sounding sea:
So pass away the cause and name
Of him who dies for Liberty!

Moore

Water Willow – **Freedom**

APRIL 25

I LIVE among the cold, the false,
   And I must seem like them;
And much I am, for I am false
   As these I most condemn:
I teach my lip its sweetest smile,
   My tongue its softest tone;
I borrow others' likeness, till
   I almost lose my own.
Chandler

White Cherry Tree – **DECEPTION**

APRIL 26

WHAT scenes appear where'er I turn my view!
The dear ideas, where I fly, pursue,
Rise in the grove, before the altar rise,
Stain all my soul, and wanton in my eyes.
I waste the matin lamp in sighs for thee;
Thy image steals between my God and me;
Thy voice I seem in every hymn to hear,
With every bead I drop too soft a tear,
When from the censer clouds of fragrance roll,
And swelling organs lift the rising soul,
One thought of thee puts all the pomp to flight –
Priests, tapers, temples, swim before my sight.
Pope

Speedwell – **'YOU ARE MY DIVINITY'**

APRIL 27

I LOOKED upon his brow – no sign
   Of guilt or fear was there;
He stood as proud by that death-shrine.
   As even o'er despair
He had a power; in his eye
There was a quenchless energy,
   A spirit that could dare
The deadliest form that death could take,
And dare it for the daring's sake.
L E L

Larch – **DARING**

APRIL 28

NEVER here, for ever there,
Free from parting, pain, and care,
Where Death and Time shall disappear
For ever *there*, but *never here*.
The timepiece of Eternity
Sayeth this incessantly –
    For ever! Never! Never! For ever!
               Longfellow

Honesty Flowers – **IMMORTALITY**

APRIL 29

HAPPY when we but seek to endure
A little pain, then find a cure,
    By double joy requited;
For friendship, like a sever'd bone,
Improves, and gains a stronger tone,
    When aptly reunited.
               Cowper

Filbert Tree – **RECONCILIATION**

APRIL 30

GO! – you may call it madness, folly,
    You shall not chase my gloom away;
There's such a charm in melancholy,
    I would not, if I could, be gay.

O! if you knew the pensive pleasure
    That fills my bosom when I sigh,
You would not rob me of a treasure
    Monarchs are too poor to buy.
               Rogers

Weeping Willow – **MELANCHOLY**

MAY

Red campion

Green hairstreak

Wallflower

Hawthorn

Herb
Robert

Sea
campion

Daisy

Pansy

Pine

MAY 1

I HARDLY know one flower that blows
  On my small garden plot;
Perhaps I may have seen a *rose,*
  And said, *Forget-me-not.*
                    Savage Landor

Forget-me-not – **'FORGET ME NOT'**

MAY 2

BUT earthly happier is the rose distilled,
Than that which, withering on the virgin thorn,
Grows, lives, and *dies* in a single blessedness.
                    Shakespeare

Saffron – **MARRIAGE**

MAY 3

THERE be more things to greet the heart and eyes
In Arno's Dome of Arts, most princely shrine,
Where Sculpture with her rainbow sister vies;
There be more marvels yet – but not for mine;
For I have been accustomed to entwine
My thoughts with Nature rather in the fields,
Than Art in galleries: though a work divine
Calls for my spirit's homage, yet it yields
Less than it feels, because the weapon which it wields
Is of another temper.

                    Byron

Acanthus – **THE FINE ARTS**

MAY 4

GIVE me a look, give me a face,
That makes simplicity a grace;
Robes loosely flowing, hair as free:
Such sweet neglect more taketh me,
Than all th' adulteries of art;
They strike mine eyes, but not my heart.
Ben Jonson

Virginian Creeper – **SWEET NEGLECT**

MAY 5

No walls were yet, nor fence, nor moat, nor mound,
Nor drum was heard, no trumpet's angry sound;
Nor swords were forged; but, void of care and crime,
The soft Creation slept away their time.
The flowers unseen in field and meadows reigned,
And western winds immortal Spring maintained;
From veins of valleys milk and nectar broke,
And honey sweating through the pores of oak.
Ovid

Beech Tree – **PROSPERITY**

MAY 6

JOY is the mainspring in the whole
    Of endless Nature's calm rotation;
Joy moves in the dazzling wheels that roll
    In the great timepiece of Creation:
Joy breathes on buds, and flowers they are;
    Joy beckons – suns come forth from heaven;
Joys rolls the spheres in realms afar;
    Ne'er to thy glass, dim Wisdom, given.
Schiller

Celandine – **JOY**

MAY 7

COME, my own heart! – none reads too oft *himself!*
Can all the stars this outward earth illume?
E'en day itself leaves half our orb in gloom:
But one lone lamp lights up the spirit's vault –
The egotist has wisdom in his fault.

Bulwer Lytton

Narcissus – **EGOTISM**

MAY 8

THE brightest gems in heaven that glow,
   Shine out from the midmost sky;
The whitest pearls of the sea below,
   In its lowest caverns lie.

He must stretch afar, who would reach a star,
   Dive deep for the pearl, I trow;
And the fairest rose that in Scotland blows,
   Hangs high on the topmost bough.

Whyte Melville

Black Thorn – **DIFFICULTY**

MAY 9

. . . . A COTTAGE snug and neat,
Upon the top of many-fountain'd Ide,
That I might thence, in holy fervour, greet
The bright-gown'd morning tripping up her side;
And when the low sun's glory-buskin'd feet
Walk on the blue wave of the Ægean tide,
Oh! I would kneel me down and worship there
The God who garnish'd out a world so bright
   and fair.

Tennant

Apple Blossom – **CHOICE**

MAY 10

LIKE the low murmur of the secret stream,
Which through dark alders winds its shaded way,
My suppliant voice is heard: ah! do not deem
That on vain toys I throw my hours away.

In the recesses of the forest vale,
On the wild mountain, on the verdant sod,
Where the fresh breezes of the morn prevail,
I wander lonely, communing with God.

Aird

Polypody Fern – **MEDITATION**

MAY 11

OH! even while he leapt, his horrid thought
Was of the peril to that lady brought;
Oh! even while he leapt, her Claud look'd back,
And shook his hand to warn her from the track.
In vain: the pleasant voice she loved so well
Feebly re-echoed through that dreadful dell, –
The voice that was the music of her home
Shouted in vain across that torrent's foam.
He saw her pausing on the bank above;
Saw – like a dreadful vision of his love –
That dazzling dream stand on the edge of death.

Hon Mrs Norton

Rhododendron – **DANGER**

MAY 12

GRACE was in all her steps, heaven in her eye,
In every gesture dignity and love.

Milton

Elm – **DIGNITY**

MAY 13

OH! who would not welcome that moment's
    returning,
  When Passion first waked a new life through his
    frame,
And his soul – like the wood that grows precious in
    burning –
  Gave out all its sweets to Love's exquisite flame.
Moore

Lilac – **FIRST EMOTIONS OF LOVE**

MAY 14

So, you see, my life is twofold.
  Half a pleasure, half a grief;
Thus all joy is somewhat temper'd,
  And all sorrow finds relief.
Adelaide Procter

Harebell – **GRIEF**

MAY 15

SPEAK of me as I am: nothing extenuate,
Nor set down aught in malice. There must you speak
Of one, that loved not wisely, but too well;
Of one not easily jealous, but, being wrought,
Perplex'd in the extreme: of one whose hand,
Like the base Judean, threw a pearl away,
Richer than all his tribe; of one whose subdu'd eyes,
Albeit unused to the melting mood,
Dropt tears as fast as the Arabian trees
Their medicinal gum. Set you down this.
Shakespeare

Chestnut – **DO ME JUSTICE**

May 16

SABRINA fair,
Listen, where thou art sitting
Under the glassy, cool, translucent wave,
In twisted braids of lilies knitting
The loose train of thy amber-dropping hair;
Listen, for dear Honor's sake,
Goddess of the silver lake, –
    Listen, and save!

Milton

Water-Lily – **INVOCATION**

May 17

HOPE comes again, to this heart long a stranger,
    Once more she sings me her flattering strain;
But hush, gentle syren! for all, there's less danger
In suffering on, than in hoping again.

Moore

Hawthorn – **HOPE**

May 18

. . . . . WHAT could I do?
Cot, garden, vineyard, and wood,
Lake, sky, and mountain, went along with him!
Could I remain behind? . . . .
. . . . I followed him
To Mantua! To breathe the air he breathed,
To walk upon the ground he walk'd upon,
To look upon the things he look'd upon,
To look, perchance, on him! – perchance to hear him –
To touch him! – never to be known to him,
Till he was told, I lived and died his love!

Sheridan Knowles

Asparagus Fern – **SECRECY**

May 19

SLIGHT withal may be the things which bring
Back on the heart the weight which it would
    fling
Aside for ever: it may be a sound,
A tone of music – summer's eve, or spring –
A flower – the wind – the ocean, which shall
    wound,
Striking the electric chain wherewith we're
    darkly bound.

Byron

Syringa – **MEMORY**

May 20

ONCE, staggering, blind with folly, on the brink of
    hell,
Above the everlasting fire-flood's frightful roar,
God threw his heart before my feet, and,
    stumbling o'er
That obstacle Divine, I into heaven fell.

Oriental

Elder – **MERCY**

May 21

HIS nature is too noble for the world;
He would not flatter Neptune for his trident,
Or Jove for his power to thunder. His heart's his
    mouth:
What his breast forges, that his tongue must vent.

Shakespeare

Osier – **CANDOUR**

MAY 22

WHY didst thou praise my humble charms,
  And, oh! then leave them to decay?
Why didst thou win me to thy arms,
  Then leave me to mourn the livelong day?

The village maidens of the plain
  Salute me lowly as they go;
Envious they mark my silken train,
  Nor think a Countess can have woe.

Mickle

Laburnum – **FORSAKEN**

....

MAY 23

RIVER of all my hopes, thou wert and art,
The current of thy being bears my heart;
Whether it sweep along in shine or shade,
By barren rocks, or banks in flowers arrayed,
Foam with the storm, or glide in soft repose.–
In that deep channel, Love unswerving flows.

Hon Mrs Norton

Bluebell – **CONSTANCY**

....

MAY 24

LOOK, nymphs and shepherds, look!
What sudden blaze of majesty
Is that we from hence descry,
Too divine to be mistook?
  This, this is she
To whom our vows and wishes bend;
  Here our solemn search hath end.

Milton

First Rose of Summer – **MAJESTY**

MAY 25

THE world goes up, and the world goes down,
 And sunshine follows the rain;
And yesterday's sneer and yesterday's frown
 Can never come over again,
 Sweet wife, –
 No, never come over again.

Charles Kingsley

Pimpernel – **CHANGE**

MAY 26

THEN a mighty gush of passion
 Through my inmost being ran;
Then my older life was ended,
 And a dearer course began.

Dearer! – oh, I cannot tell thee
 What a load was swept away, –
What a world of doubt and darkness
 Faded in the dawning day.

Aytoun

Lily of the Valley – **RETURN OF HAPPINESS**

MAY 27

BUT now he stood, chained and alone,
 The headsman by his side,
The plume, the helm, the charger gone;
 The sword which had defied
The mightiest, lay broken near;
And yet no sign, no sound of fear,
 Came from that lip of pride;
And never king or conqueror's brow
Wore higher look than his did now.

L E L

Poplar – **COURAGE**

MAY 28

LOVE thee? – so well, so tenderly,
  Thou'rt loved, adored, by me,
Fame, fortune, wealth, and liberty,
  Are worthless without thee!
Moore

Red Tulip – **CONFESSION OF LOVE**

MAY 29

BLEST be that spot, where cheerful guests retire
To pause from toil, and trim their evening fire;
Blest that abode, where want and pain repair,
And every stranger finds a ready chair.
Blest be those feasts, with simple plenty
    crown'd,
Where all the ruddy family around
Laugh at the jests or pranks, that never fail,
Or sigh with pity at some mournful tale,
Or press the bashful stranger to his food,
And learn the luxury of doing good.
Goldsmith

Oak – **HOSPITALITY**

MAY 30

SOMETIMES, with secure delight,
The upland hamlets will invite,
When the merry bells ring round,
And the jocund rebecks sound,
To many a youth, and many a maid,
Dancing in the chequer'd shade.
Milton

Sothernwood – **MERRIMENT**

MAY 31

FAME is the spur that the clear spirit doth raise
(That last infirmity of noble minds)
So scorn delights, and live laborious days;
But the fair guerdon when we hope to find,
And think to burst out into sudden blaze,
Comes the blind Fury with th'abhorrèd shears,
And slits the thin-spun life.

Milton

Tulip Tree – **FAME**

JUNE

Iris

Small heath

Helen Traubel

Boursault (rose)

Hybrid tea (rose)

Rugosa

Great bindweed

JUNE 1

BUT never yet, by night or day,
In dew of spring, or summer's ray,
Did the sweet Valley shine so gay
As now it shines, all love and light,
Visions by day, and feasts by night!
A happier smile illumes each brow,
    With quicker spread each heart uncloses,
And all is ecstacy, – for now
    The Valley holds its Feast of Roses.

Moore

Rose (Gloire de Dijon) – **GLADNESS**

JUNE 2

So a fresh and glad emotion
    Rose within my swelling breast,
And I hurried swiftly onwards,
    To the haven of my rest.

Thou wert there with word and welcome,
    With thy smile so purely sweet;
And I laid my heart before thee,
    Laid it, darling, at thy feet.

Aytoun

Rose (Apricot) – **'WELCOME ME'**

JUNE 3

'Go, gentle Muse! and when my anthems rise,
Where Heaven's loud chorus charms the list'ning skies,
One thankful strain shall yet remember thee!'
She ceased; and thus her wish my answer crown'd:
'Prompt at thy will, and to thy orders bound,
Thy faithful delegate, thy servant, see!
Spirit benign! whose disentangled soul
Thy brethren taught to spurn the nether goal,
Pierce the blue mundane shell, and claim the sky;
Such energy attend thy warm request,
That my strong wish outruns my winged haste,
Nor need you more your holy influence try.'

Dante

Rose (Cabbage) – **AMBASSADOR**

JUNE 4

. . . . . WHEN we love,
All air breathes music, like the branchy bower,
By Indian bards feign'd, which, with ceaseless
        song,
Answers the sun's bright raylets; nor till eve
Folds her melodious leaves, and all night rests,
Drinking deep draughts of silence.

Bailey

Rose (Boursault) – **HAPPY LOVE**

JUNE 5

ON her white breast a sparkling cross she wore,
Which Jews might kiss, and infidels adore;
Her lively looks, and sprightly mind disclose,
Quick as her eyes, and as unfix'd as those.
Favours to none, to all she smiles extends,
Oft she rejects, but never once offends.
Bright as the sun, her eyes the gazer strike
And like the sun they shine on all alike.
Yet graceful ease, and sweetness void of pride,
Might hide her faults, if belles had faults to hide;
If to her share some female errors fall,
Look in her face, and you'll forget them all.

Pope

Rose (Austrian) – '**THOU ART ALL THAT IS LOVELY**'

JUNE 6

SEE virgin Eve, with graces bland,
Fresh blooming from her Maker's hand,
    In Orient beauty beam!
Fair on the river-margin laid,
She knew not that her image made
    The angel in the stream.

Logan

Rose (Burgundy) – **UNCONSCIOUSNESS**

JUNE 7

WHETHER joy danced in her dark eye,
Or woe or pity claim'd a sigh,
Or filial love was glowing there,
Or meek devotion pour'd a prayer,
Or tale of injury call'd forth
Th' indignant spirit of the North, –
One only passion unreveal'd.
With maiden pride, the maid conceal'd,
Yet not less purely felt the flame; –
Oh! need I tell that passion's name?

Scott

Rose (Unique) – **MODESTY**

JUNE 8

OH! fair as the sea-flower close to thee growing,
Like the wind of the south o'er a summer lute
    blowing,
But long upon Araby's green sunny highlands
    Shall maids and their lovers remember the
        doom
Of her, who lies sleeping among the pearl
    islands,
    With nought but the sea-star to light up her
        tomb.

Moore

Rose (Caroline) – **LOVE IS DANGEROUS**

JUNE 9

UNTUTOR'D by science, a stranger to fear
    And rude as the rocks where my infancy grew,
No feeling save one to my bosom was dear
    Need I say, my sweet Mary, 'twas center'd in
        you?
Yet it could not be love, for I knew not the
        name –
    What passion can dwell in the heart of a child?
But still I perceive an emotion the same
    As I felt when a boy, on the crag-cover'd wild.

Byron

Rosebud (White) – **A HEART IGNORANT OF LOVE**

June 10

Beauty is but a vain and doubtful good,
A shining gloss that fadeth suddenly;
A flower that dies when first it 'gins to bud;
A brittle glass that's broken presently:
A doubtful good, a gloss, a glass, a flower,
Lost, faded, broken, dead within an hour!

Shakespeare

Rose (Red-leaved) – **Beauty**

June 11

They seem'd all fair, – but there was one,
On whom the light had not yet shone,
Or shone but partly; so downcast
She held her brow as slow she pass'd.
And yet to me there seem'd to dwell
About that unseen face –
A something in the shade that fell
Over that brow's imagined grace –
Which won me more than all the best
Outshining beauties of the rest.

Moore

Rose (China) – **Grace**

June 12

'Tell me my fate!' he cried, seizing her hand;
'Thy fate?' she answered, 'tell me rather mine!
Bend pride's stiff knees; no longer grace
    withstand,
And I will be for ever, ever thine!
If not, then Heaven hath this dear bounty
    bann'd,
And my poor heart must thy rich heart resign.
I am Madonna's child, come life what may;
Come death – O! Godfrid, kneel with me, and
    pray!'

Austin

Rose (Rambler) – **'Only deserve my love'**

June 13

COME, thou whose thoughts as limpid
    streams are clear,
To lead the train – sweet Modesty, appear!
Here make thy court, amidst our rural scene,
And shepherd girls shall own thee for their
    Queen.

Collins

Rose (Deep Red) – **BASHFULNESS**

....

June 14

ASK me not how much I love thee –
    Do not question why;
        I have told thee the tale,
        In the evening pale,
    With a tear and a sigh.

Oh, a king would have loved and left thee,
    And away thy sweet love cast;
        But I am thine,
        Whilst the stars shall shine –
    To the last – to the last!

Barry Cornwall

Rosebud (Moss) – **CONFESSION OF LOVE**

....

June 15

WELL had he learn'd to curb the crowd,
By arts that veil, and oft preserve the proud;
His was the lofty port, the distant mien,
That seems to shun the sight – and awes, if seen;
The solemn aspect, and the high-born eye,
That checks low mirth, but lacks not courtesy.

Scott

Rose (Holy) – **PRIDE**

....

June 16

.... Overtasked at length.
Both Love and Hope beneath the load give way;
Then, with a statue's smile, a statue's strength,
Stands the mute sister, Patience, nothing loth,
And both supporting, does the work of both.
Coleridge

Rose (Moss) – **Superior Merit**

June 17

Farewell, farewell! but this I tell
    To thee, thou wedding guest:
He prayeth well, who loveth well
    Both man, and bird, and beast.

He prayeth best, who loveth best
    All things, both great and small;
For the dear God who loveth us,
    He made and loveth all.
Coleridge

Rose (Virginian) – **Compassion**

June 18

This – this shall be a consecrated spot;
But *thou* – when all that birth and beauty throws
Of magic round thee is extinct – shall have
One-half the laurel that oe'rshades my grave.
No power in death can tear our names apart,
As none in life could rend thee from my heart.
Yes, Leonora! it shall be our fate
To be entwined for ever – but too late!
Byron

Rose (Lancaster) – **Union**

June 19

WHEN fix'd in Memory's mirror dwells
  Some dear-loved form, to fleet no more,
Transformed, as by Arabian spells,
  We catch the likeness we adore:
Then, ah! who would not love most true?
Who would not be in love with you?

Keble

Cluster Rose – '**YOU ARE CHARMING**'

June 20

WHEN Gracia, beautiful but faithless fair,
  Who long in passion's bonds my heart had kept,
First with false blushes pitied my despair,
  I smiled with pleasure! – should I not have wept?

And when, to gratify some wealthier wight,
  She left to grief the heart she had beguiled.
The heart grew sick, and, saddening at the sight,
  I wept with sorrow! – should I not have
    smiled?

Moncrieff

Rose (Musk) – **A CAPRICIOUS BEAUTY**

June 21

MAIDEN with the meek brown eyes,
In whose orbs a shadow lies,
Like the dusk in evening skies;
Thou whose locks outshine the sun,
Golden tresses wreathed in one.
As the braided streamlets run!
Standing with reluctant feet,
Where the brook and river meet,
Womanhood and childhood fleet.

Longfellow

Rosebud (Red) – '**YOU ARE YOUNG AND BEAUTIFUL**'

June 22

CALL back the dew
    That on the rose at morn was lying;
When the day is dying,
    Bid the sunbeam stay;
Call back the wave,
    E'en while the ebbing tide's receding;
Oh! all unheeding
    Of thy voice are they!
As vain the call
    Distraction makes on love departed;
When the broken-hearted
    Bitter tears let fall.

Charles Dickens

Rose (Yellow) – **DEPARTURE OF LOVE**

June 23

Is it, O man, with such discordant noises,
    With such accursed instruments as these,
Thou drownest Nature's sweet and kindly voices,
    And jarrest the celestial harmonies?

Were half the power that fills the world with terror,
    Were half the wealth bestow'd on camps and
        courts,
Given to redeem the human mind from error,
    There were no need of arsenals nor forts.

Longfellow

Rose (York) – **WAR**

June 24

How can we live so far apart?
Oh! why not rather, heart to heart,
    United live and die?
Like those sweet birds, that fly together,
With feather always touching feather,
    Link'd by a hook and eye!

Moore

Rose (White and Red) – **UNITY**

June 25

HER form was as the morning's blightsome star,
　That, capp'd with lustrous coronet of beams,
Rides up the dawning orient in her car,
　New wash'd, and doubly 'fulgent from the
　　streams.
The Caldee shepherd eyes her light afar,
　And on his knees adores her as she gleams:
So shone the stately form of Maggie Launder,
And so the admiring crowds pay homage and
　applaud her.

Tennant

Rose (Damask) – **FRESHNESS**

June 26

ASK what prevailing, pleasing power
　Allures the sportive, wandering bee
To roam untired from flower to flower;
　He'll tell you, 'tis variety.

Look Nature round, her features trace,
　Her seasons, all her changes see;
And own, upon Creation's face
　The greatest charm's variety.

Moore

Rose (Mundi) – **VARIETY**

June 27

LADY, do not heed her warning;
　Trust me, thou shalt find me true;
Constant as the light of morning
　I will ever be to you.

Lady, I will not deceive thee,
　Fill thy guileless heart with woe;
Trust me, lady, and believe me,
　Sorrow thou shalt never know.

Manahan

Rose (White) – **'I AM WORTHY OF YOU'**

June 28

. . . . . It were all one,
That I should love a bright particular star,
And think to wed it. He is so above me,
In his bright radiance and collateral light
Must I be comforted, not in his sphere.
The ambition in my love thus plagues itself:
The hind that would be mated with the lion
Must die for love.

Shakespeare

Rose (Maiden Blush) – **Timid Love**

June 29

To kneel at many a shrine,
    Yet lay the heart on none;
To think all other charms divine,
    But those we just have won; –
This is love, faithless love,
Such as kindleth hearts that rove.

Moore

Rose (White Withered) – **Transient Impressions**

June 30

So dear to Heaven is saintly chastity,
That when a soul is found sincerely so,
A thousand liveried angels lacquey her,
Driving far off each thing of sin and guilt,
And in clear dream, and solemn vision,
Tell her of things, that no gross ear can hear;
Till oft converse with heavenly habitants,
Begin to cast a beam on th' outward shape,
The unpolluted temple of the mind,
And turns it by degrees to the soul's essence,
Till all be made immortal.

Milton

Crown of Roses – **Reward of Chastity**

JULY

Foxglove

Ringlet

Bracken

Honeysuckle

Field poppy

Hoary plantain

Bell heather

July 1

Young Henry was as brave a youth
  As ever graced a martial story;
And Jane was fair as lovely truth:
  She sigh'd for Love, and he for Glory.

With her his faith he meant to plight,
  And told her many a gallant story;
Till war, their coming joys to blight,
  Call'd him away from Love to Glory.

Young Henry met the foe with pride,
  Jane followed, fought – ah! hapless story! –
In man's attire, by Henry's side;
  She died for Love, and he for Glory.

Dibdin

Pink (Carnation) – **Boldness**

July 2

Fair girl! by whose simplicity
  My spirit has been won
From the stern earthliness of life,
  As shadows flee the sun;

I turn again to think of thee,
  And half deplore the thought,
That for one instance o'er my soul
  Forgetfulness hath wrought!

I turn to that charm'd hour of hope,
  When first upon my view
Came the pure sunshine of thine heart,
  Borne from thine eyes of blue.

Willis Clarke

White Lily – **Purity**

July 3

Adieu, adieu! my native land
  Fades o'er the waters blue;
The night-winds sigh, the breakers roar,
  And shrieks the wild sea-mew.

Yon sun that sets upon the sea,
  We follow in his flight;
Farewell awhile to him and thee:
  My native land – good-night!

Byron

Sweet Pea – **Departure**

July 4

Alas! the love of women! it is known
    To be a lovely and a fearful thing;
For all of theirs upon that die is thrown,
    And if 'tis lost, life has no more to bring
To them, but mockeries of the past alone.
Byron

Carnation – **Woman's Love**

July 5

But if ye saw that which no eyes can see,
The inward beauty of her lively sp'rit,
Garnish'd with heavenly gifts of high degree,
Much more would ye wonder at that sight,
And stand astonish'd, like to those which read
Medusa's mazeful head.
There dwells sweet love and constant chastity,
Unspotted faith, and comely womanhood,
Regard of honour, and mild modesty;
There Virtue reigns as queen on royal throne,
And giveth laws alone,
The which the base affections do obey,
And yield their services unto her will.
Spenser

Mignonette – **Excellence**

July 6

Go, blushing flower!
And tell her this from me,
    That in the bower
    From which I gathered thee,
At evening I will be.
Peter Spencer

Iris – **'I have a message for you'**

July 7

Lo! she cometh in her beauty,
 Stately, with a Juno grace,
Raven locks, Madonna-braided,
 O'er her sweet and blushing face;

Eyes of deepest violet, beaming
 With the love that knows not shame;
Lips that thrill my inmost being,
 With the utterance of a name!

Aytoun

Imperial Lily – **Dignity**

July 8

Mine is the charm whose mystic sway
The spirits of past delight obey;
Let but the tuneful talisman sound,
And they come like genii hovering round.
And mine is the gentle song, that bears
From soul to soul the wishes of love;
As a bird, that wafts through genial airs
The cinnamon seed from grove to grove.
'Tis I that mingle, in one sweet measure,
The past, the present, and future of pleasure.

Moore

Verbena – **Enchantment**

July 9

A mirthful man he was – the snows of age
Fell, but they did not chill him: gaiety,
Even in life's closing, touch'd his teeming brain,
With such visions as the setting sun
Raises in front of some hoar glacier,
Painting the bleak ice with a thousand hues.

Scott

Guelder Rose – **Growing Old**

July 10

WHEN slumber first unclouds my brain,
　And thought is free,
And sense, refresh'd, renews her reign, –
　I think of thee.

When, next, in prayer to God above
　I bend my knee,
Then, when I pray for those I love, –
　I pray for thee.

In short, one only wish I have –
　To live for thee;
Or gladly, if one pang 'twould save,
　I'd die for thee.

Anon

Red Double Pink – **ARDENT LOVE**

July 11

IT is a flame, an ardour of the mind,
Dead in the proper corpse, quick in another's;
Transfers the lover into the loved.
That he or she that loves, engraves or stamps
The idea of what they love, first in themselves;
Or life to glasses, so their minds take in
The forms of their beloved, and them reflect.
It is the likeness of affections.

Ben Jonson

Acacia – **CHASTE LOVE**

July 12

GIVE me more love, or more disdain:
　The torrid or the frozen zone
Bring equal ease unto my pain –
　The temperate affords me none.
Either extreme of love or hate,
Is sweeter than a calm estate.

Carew

Striped Carnation – **EXTREMES**

July 13

HAST thou found naught within thy troubled life,
    Save inward strife?
Hast thou found all he promised thee deceit,
    And hope a cheat?
Endure, – and there shall dawn within thy heart
    Eternal rest.

Young

Scarlet Geranium – **COMFORT**

July 14

'FAITHLESS Paris! cruel Paris!'
    Thus the poor deserted spake –
'Wherefore thus so strangely leave me?
    Why thy loving bride forsake?
Why no tender word at parting –
    Why no kiss, no farewell take?
Would that I could but forget thee!
    Would this throbbing heart might
        break.

Aytoun

Lotus Flower – **ESTRANGED LOVE**

July 15

SHE who only finds her self-esteem
In others' admiration, begs an alms:
Depends on others for her daily food,
And is the very servant of her slaves;
Though oftentimes, in a fantastic hour,
O'er men she might a childish power exert,
Which not ennobles, but degrades her state.

Joanna Baillie

Day Lily – **COQUETRY**

July 16

THE charms of eloquence – the skill
 To wake each secret string,
And from the bosom's chords at will
 Life's mournful music bring;
The o'ermast'ring strength of mind which sways
 The haughty and the free,
Whose might earth's mightiest ones obey –
 This charm was given to – thee.

Mrs Embury

Lotus – **ELOQUENCE**

July 17

PLEASANT were many scenes; but most to me,
The solitude of vast extent, untouched
By hand of art, where Nature sowed herself,
And reaped her crops; whose garments were the clouds;
Whose minstrels brooks, whose lamps the moon and stars;
Whose organ choir the voice of many waters;
Whose banquets morning dews; whose heroes storms;
Whose warriors mighty winds; whose lovers, flowers;
Whose orators the thunderbolts of God;
Whose palaces the everlasting hills;
Whose ceiling heaven's unfathomable blue.

Pollock

Magnolia – **LOVE OF NATURE**

July 18

BRIGHT as the pillar rose at Heaven's command,
When Israel march'd along the desert land,
Blazed through the night of lonely wilds afar,
And told the path – a never-setting star:
So, heavenly Genius, in thy course divine,
Hope is the star, her light is ever thine.

Campbell

Ivy-leaved Geranium – **GENIUS**

July 19

At morn, beside yon summer sea,
    Young Hope and Love reclined;
But scarce had noon-tide come, when he
Into his bark leap'd smilingly,
    And left poor Hope behind.

'I go', said Love, 'to sail awhile
    Across this sunny main:'
And then, so sweet his parting smile,
That Hope, who never dreamt of guile,
    Believed he'd come again.

Now fast around the sea and shore
    Night threw her darkling chain;
The sunny sails were seen no more,
Hope's morning dreams of bliss were o'er –
Love never came again.

Moore

Convolvolus – **Extinguished Hope**

July 20

What shall we call it, folly or good nature?
So soft, so simple, and so kind a creature?
When Charity so blindly plays its part,
It only shows the weakness of her heart.

Terence

White Jasmine – **Extreme Amiability**

July 21

False World, thou ly'st: thou canst not lend
    The least delight;
Thy favours cannot gain a friend,
    They are so slight;
Thy morning pleasures make an end,
    To please at night:
Poor are the arts that thou supply'st,
And yet thou vaunt'st, and yet thou vy'st
With Heaven: fond Earth, thou boasts; false
        World, thou ly'st.

Quarles

Yellow Lily – **Falsehood**

July 22

OH! my love has an eye of the softest blue,
　Yet it was not that that won me;
But a bright little drop from the soul was there,
　'Tis *that* that has undone me:
I might have forgotten that red, red lip –
　Yet how from the thought to sever?
But there was a smile from the sunshine within,
And that smile I'll remember for ever.

Wolfe

Larkspur – **BRIGHTNESS**

July 23

THOUGHTLESS of beauty, she was Beauty's self,
Recluse among the close embowering woods;
As in the hollow breast of Appenine,
Beneath the shelter of encircling hills,
A myrtle rises far from human eyes,
And breathes its balmy fragrance o'er the wild;
So flourish'd, blooming and unseen by all,
The sweet Lavinia.

Thomson

Honeysuckle – **RUSTIC BEAUTY**

July 24

How oft my guardian angel gently cried,
'Soul, from thy casement look, and thou shalt see
How he persists to knock and wait for thee.'
And oh! how often to that voice of sorrow,
'To-morrow we will open,' I replied;
And when the morrow came, I answered still,
　'To-morrow!'

Vega

Balsam – **IMPATIENCE**

July 25

No tears, Celia, now shall win
    My resolved heart to return;
I have search'd thy soul within,
    And find nought but pride and scorn.
I have learn'd thy arts, and now
Can disdain as much as thou.
Some power, in my revenge, convey
That love to her I cast away.

Carew

Yellow Carnation – **Disdain**

July 26

Her face was as the summer cloud, whereon
The dawning sun delights to rest his rays;
Compared with it, old Sharon's vale, o'er-grown
With flaunting roses, had resign'd its praise.

Her locks, apparent tufts of wiry gold,
Lay on her lily temples, fairly dangling;
And on each hair, so harmless to behold,
A lover's soul hung mercilessly strangling;
The piping silly zephyrs vied to enfold
The tresses in their arms so slim and tangling,
And thrid in sport these lover-noosing snares,
And played at hide-and-seek amid the golden-hairs.

Tennant

White Pink – **'You are fair and fascinating'**

July 27

So long thy power hath blest me, sure it still will lead
    me on,
O'er moor and fen, o'er crag and torrent, till the night
    is gone;
And with the morn those angel faces smile,
Which I have loved long since, and lost awhile.

Newman

Passion Flower – **Belief**

July 28

'Oh Love!' said I, in thoughtless mood,
  As deep I drank of Lethe's stream,
'Be all my sorrows in this flood
  Forgotten, like a vanish'd dream!'

But who could bear that gloomy blank,
  Where joy was lost, as well as pain?
Quickly of Memory's fount I drank,
  And brought the past all back again;

And said, 'O Love! whate'er my lot,
  Still let this soul to thee be true, –
Rather than have one bliss forgot,
  Be all my pains remember' too!'

Moore

Knotweed – **Recantation**

July 29

There is a love, which is not the love only
Of the thoughtless and the young; there is a love
      which sees
Not with the eye, which hears not with
The ears; but in which soul is enamoured
Of soul: it is a love only high
And noble natures can conceive, – it hath nothing
In common with the sympathies and ties
Of coarse affection.

Bulwer Lytton

Acacia (Rose) – **Platonic Love**

July 30

Ho! all who labour, all who strive,
  Ye wield a lofty power;
Do with your might, do with your strength,
  Fill every golden hour:
The glorious privilege, to do,
  Is man's most noble dower!
Oh, to your birthright and yourselves,
  To your own souls be true!
A weary, wretched life is theirs,
  Who have no work to do.

Orme

Bee Orchis – **Industry**

July 31

I NEVER loved ambitiously to climb,
Or trust my hand too far into the fire.
To be in heaven, sure, is a blessed thing;
But, Atlas-like, to prop heaven on one's back,
Cannot but be more labour than delight.
Such is the state of men in honour placed;
They are gold vessels made for servile uses;
High trees, that keep the weather from low houses,
But cannot shield the tempest from themselves.

Nash

Mountain Pink – **AMBITION**

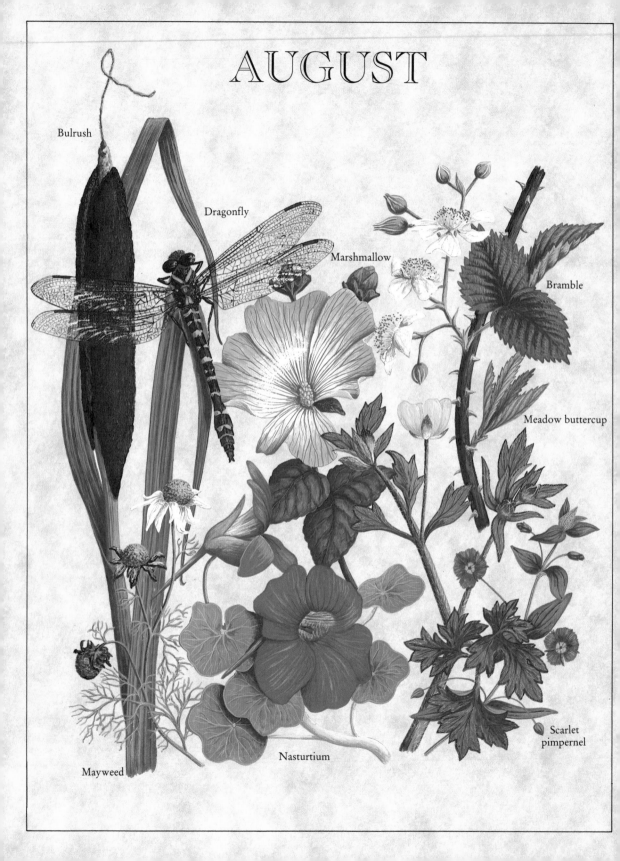

AUGUST

Bulrush

Dragonfly

Marshmallow

Bramble

Meadow buttercup

Scarlet
pimpernel

Nasturtium

Mayweed

August 1

Can gold calm passion, or make reason shine?
Can we dig peace or wisdom from the mine?
Wisdom to gold prefer, for 'tis much less
To make our fortune than our happiness:
That happiness which great ones see,
With rage and wonder in a low degree,
Themselves unbless'd: the poor are only poor,
But what are they who droop amid their store?
Nothing is meaner that a wretch of state;
The happy only are the truly great.

Young

Corn – **Riches**

August 2

O away! my thoughts are earthward!
    Not asleep, my love, art thou!
Dwelling in the land of glory
    With the saints and angels now.

Brighter, fairer far than living,
    With no trace of woe or pain,
Robed in everlasting beauty,
    Shall I see thee once again,

By the light that never fadeth,
    Underneath eternal skies,
When the dawn of Resurrection
    Breaks o'er deathless Paradise.

Aytoun

Field Red Poppy – **Consolation**

August 3

Full on the casement shone the wintry moon,
And threw warm gules on Madeline's fair breast,
As down she knelt for Heaven's grace and boon;
Rose-bloom fell on her hands, together press'd,
And on her silver cross soft amethyst,
And on her hair a glory like a saint;
She seem'd a splendid angel newly drest,
Save wings, for Heaven:– Porphyro grew faint!
She knelt, so pure a thing, so free from mortal taint.

Keats

Corn Flower – **Purity**

August 4

Warm curtain'd was the little bed,
Soft pillow'd was the little head;
'The storm will wake the child,' they said:
    Miserere Domine!

Cowering among the pillows white,
He prays, his blue eyes dim with fright:
'Father, save those at sea to-night!' –
    Miserere Domine!

The morning shone, all clear and gay,
On a ship at anchor in the bay,
And on a little child at play, –
    Gloria tibi, Domine!
        Adelaide Procter

Traveller's Joy – **Safety**

August 5

I pant for the music which is divine,
    My heart in its thirst is a dying flower;
Pour forth the sound like enchanted wine,
    Loosen the notes in a silver shower:
Like a herbless plain for the gentle rain,
I gasp, I faint, till they wake again.

Let me drink of the spirit of that sweet sound –
    More, O, more! I am thirsting yet;
It loosens the serpent which care has bound
    Upon my heart, to stifle it;
The dissolving strain, through every vein,
Passes into my heart and brain.
        Shelley

Oats – **Music**

August 6

Elysium shall be thine; the blissful plains
Of utmost earth, where Rhadamanthus reigns;
Joys ever young, unmix'd with pain or fear,
Fill the wide circle of th' eternal year.
Stern Winter smiles in that auspicious clime,
The fields are florid with unfading prime;
From the bleak pole no winds inclement blow,
Mould the round hail, or flake the fleecy snow;
But from the breezy deep the blest inhale
The fragrant murmur of the western gale.
        Pope's 'Homer'

Wheat – **Prosperity**

AUGUST 7

COME, gentle Sleep! attend thy votary's prayer,
And, though Death's image, to my couch repair:
How sweet, though lifeless, yet with life to lie;
And without dying, oh how sweet to die!
Thomas Warton

White Poppy – **SLEEP**

AUGUST 8

BE kind and courteous to this gentleman,
Hop in his walks, and gambol in his eyes;
Feed him with apricots and dewberries,
With purple grapes, green figs, and mulberries;
The honey-bags steal from the humble bees,
And for night tapers crop their waxen thighs,
And light them at the fiery glowworm's eyes,
To have my love to bed, and to arise;
And pluck the wings of painted butterflies,
To fan the moonbeams from his sleeping eyes.
Shakespeare

Pink Geranium – **PARTIALITY**

AUGUST 9

. . . . HE is in love with an ideal;
A creature of his own imagination;
A child of air; an echo of his heart;
And, like a lily on a river floating,
She floats upon the river of his thoughts.
Longfellow

Crimson Poppy – **FANTASY**

August 10

THE maiden paused, as if again
She thought to hear the distant strain;
With head upraised, and look intent,
And eye and ear attentive bent,
And locks flung back, and lips apart.
Like monument of Grecian art;
In listening mood she seem'd to stand,
The guardian Naiad of the strand:
And ne'er did Grecian chisel trace
A nymph, a Naiad, or a grace,
Of finer form or lovelier face.

Scott

Yellow Jasmine – **GRACE AND ELEGANCE**

August 11

THOU wert still the Lady Flora,
   In the morning garb of bloom:
Where thou wert was light and glory,
   Where thou wert not, dearth and gloom.

So for many days I follow'd,
   For a long and weary while,
Ere my heart rose up to bless thee,
   For the yielding of a smile.

Aytoun

Oak-leaved Geranium – **'LADY, DEIGN TO SMILE.'**

August 12

FROM a dark cloud a drop of rain
   Was falling, when, alas! ashamed
As it approach'd the boundless main,
   In woful accents it exclaim'd:
'How wide! how vast! ah me, forlorn!
   With *that* compared, I am but naught':
While thus it view'd itself with scorn,
   A shell it in its bosom caught;
Thus conscious of its humble state,
   'Twas changed into a brilliant gem
An orient pearl – and raised by fate
   To deck the brightest diadem.

Oriental

Broom – **HUMILITY**

August 13

THAT grace and elegance, so rarely seen;
That voice, which in the inmost soul is felt;
That air inspired, that heavenly gait and mien;
Those eyes, whose glance the proudest heart
    can melt;
Her words, where mind, and thought, and
    genius shine;
Her silence sweet, her manners all divine.

Petrarch

Indian Double Pink – **ALWAYS LOVELY**

August 14

THEN from Olympian tops, in wrath,
Apollo took his downward path;
Well closed and fit his quiver hung,
And as like night he swept along,
The darts upon his shoulders rang,
The silver bow gave deadly clang.
He sat him from the ships apart,
Then issued forth the bitter dart;
Fleet dogs and mules at first he slew,
And next upon the men he drew;
And, as he shot, unnumber'd fires
Stream'd upwards from the funeral pyres.

Popes 'Homer'

Peony – **ANGER**

August 15

BUT, O my first, O my best, I could not choose but
    love thee;
O, to be a wild white bird, and seek thy rocky
    bed!
From my breast I'd give thee burial, pluck the
    down, and spread above thee;
I would sit and sing thy requiem on the mountain
    head.
Fare thee well, my love of loves! would I had died
    before thee!

Jean Ingelow

Asphodel – **'MY REGRETS FOLLOW YOU TO THE GRAVE.'**

AUGUST 16

THEN wilt thou remember what now seems to pass
Like the moonlight on water, the breath-stain on
    glass;
O, maiden the lovely and youthful! to thee
How rose-touch'd the page of thy future must be!
L E L

Coral Honeysuckle – 'THE COLOUR OF MY FATE.'

AUGUST 17

O MAIDEN fair! O maiden fair!
    How faithless is thy bosom –
To love me in prosperity
And leave me in adversity!
O maiden fair! O maiden fair!
    How faithless is thy bosom!

The nightingale, the nightingale
    Thou tak'st for thine example:
So long as summer laughs she sings,
But in the autumn spreads her wings:
The nightingale, the nightingale
    Thou tak'st for thine example.
Longfellow

Monkshood – FICKLENESS

AUGUST 18

LIKE one who, some imagined peril near,
Feels his warm wishes chill'd by wintry fear,
    And resolution sicken at the view;
Thus I perceived my sinking spirits fail,
Thus trembling I survey'd the gloomy vale,
    As near the moment of decision drew.
Dante

Quaking Grass – AGITATION

August 19

Is man more just than God? is man more pure
Than He who dreams even seraphs insecure!
Creatures of clay – vain dwellers in the dust!
The moth survives you, and are ye more just?
Things of a day! you wither ere the night,
Heedless and blind to Wisdom's wasted light!

Byron

Snapdragon – **PRESUMPTION**

August 20

ANOTHER nymph, amongst the many fair
That made my softer hours their solemn care,
Before the rest affected still to stand,
And watch'd my eye, preventing my command.
Abra – she so was call'd – did soonest haste
To grace my presence; Abra went the last.
Abra was ready ere I call'd her name;
And though I call'd another, Abra came.

Prior

Stock – **PROMPTITUDE**

August 21

THERE *was* a time when bliss
Shone o'er thy heart from every look of his;
When but to see him, hear him, breathe the air
In which he dwelt, was thy soul's fondest prayer;
When round him hung such a perpetual spell,
Whate'er he did, none ever did so well.
Too happy days! when, if he touch'd a flower
Or gem of thine, 'twas sacred from that hour!

Moore

Alkanet – **DEVOTION**

August 22

THE heart that has truly loved never forgets,
But as truly loves on to the close,
As the sunflower turns to her god, when he sets,
The same look that she gave when he rose.

Moore

Sunflower – **ADORATION**

······································

August 23

No real Poet ever wove in numbers
All his dream; but the diviner part,
Hidden from all the world, spake to him only,
In the voiceless silence of his heart.

So with Love; for Love and Art united
Are twin mysteries – different, yet the same:
Poor indeed would be the love of any,
Who could find its full and perfect name.

Adelaide Procter

Banksia – **LOVE SWEET AND SILENT**

······································

August 24

ALAS! they had been friends in youth,
But whispering tongues can poison truth;
And consistancy lives in realms above,
And life is thorny, and youth is vain;
And to be wroth with one we love,
Doth work like madness in the brain.

Coleridge

Madagasgar Jasmine – **SEPARATION**

······································

August 25

.... I CANNOT flatter; I do defy
The tongues of soothers; but a braver place
In my heart's love, hath no man than yourself.
Shakespeare

SWEET, sweet is flattery to mortal ears;
And if I drink thy praise too greedily,
My fault I'll match with grosser instances:
Do not the royal souls that van the world
Hunger for praise? does not the hero burn
To blow his triumphs in the trumpet's mouth?
And do not poets' brows throb feverous,
Till they are cool'd with laurels?
Smith

Venus's Looking-glass – **FLATTERY**

August 26

UNTIL I loved I was alone:
I asked too much of intellect and grace,
To pine, though young, for every pretty face,
Whose passing brightness to quick fancies made
A sort of sunshine in the idle shade;
Beauties who starr'd the earth like common flowers,
The careless eglantines of wayside bowers.
I lingered till some blossom rich and rare
Hung like a glory on the scented air,
Enamouring at once the heart and eye,
So that I paused, and could not pass it by;
Then woke the passionate love within my heart,
And only with my life shall that depart.
Hon Mrs Norton

Clematis – **MENTAL BEAUTY**

August 27

THEN, is the past so gloomy now,
    That it may never bear
The open smile of Nature's brow,
    Or meet the sunny air?

I know not that – but joy is power,
    However short it last;
And joy befits the present hour,
    If sadness fits the past.
Aytoun

Red Dahlia – **JOY**

AUGUST 28

THE time I've lost in wooing,
In watching and pursuing
   The light that lies
   In woman's eyes,
Has been my heart's undoing.

Though Wisdom oft has sought me,
I scorn'd the lore she brought me
   My only books
   Were woman's looks,
And folly's all they've taught me.

Moore

Pomegranate – **FOLLY**

AUGUST 29

YE see yon birkie, ca'd a lord,
   Wha struts, and stares, and a' that;
Though hundreds worship at his word,
   He's but a coof for a' that.
For a' that, and a' that,
The man of independent mind,
   He looks and laughs at a' that.

Burns

Borage – **BLUNTNESS**

AUGUST 30

THE wise and active conquer difficulties,
By daring to attempt them; Sloth, and Folly
Shiver and shrink at sight of toil and hazard,
And make the impossibility they fear.

Rowe

Camomile – **ENERGY IN ADVERSITY**

August 31

I BRING thee, love, a golden chain,
  I bring thee, too, a flowery wreath.

The chain is form'd of golden threads,
  Bright as Minerva's yellow hair,
When the last beam of evening sheds
  Its calm and sober lustre there.

The wreath of brightest myrtle wove,
  With sun-lit drops of bliss among it,
And many a rose-leaf cull'd by love,
  To heal his lip when bees have stung it.
Come, tell me which the tie shall be,
To bind thy gentle heart to me?

Moore

Monthly Honeysuckle – **BOND OF LOVE**

SEPTEMBER

Bracken

Small heath

Shasta daisy

Tutsan

Tormentil

Bramble

SEPTEMBER 1

WHERE your soul is tempted
Most to trust your fate,
Then with double caution
Linger, fear, and wait.
Adelaide Procter

Apple – **TEMPTATION**

SEPTEMBER 2

HAS sorrow thy young days shaded,
As clouds o'er the morning fleet?
Too fast have those young days faded,
That even in sorrow were sweet!
Does Time with his cold wing wither
Each feeling that once was dear? –
Then, child of misfortune, come hither;
I'll weep with thee tear for tear.
Moore

Aloe – **SORROW**

SEPTEMBER 3

IN peasant life he might have known
As fair a face, as sweet a tone;
But village notes could ne'er supply
That rich and varied melody;
And ne'er in cottage maid was seen
The easy dignity of mien,
Claiming respect, yet waiving state,
That marks the daughters of the great.
Scott

Geranium (White) – **REFINEMENT**

SEPTEMBER 4

YET not by fetter nor by spear
   His sovereignty was held or won;
Feared – but alone as freemen fear,
   Loved – but as freemen love alone;
He waved the sceptre o'er his kind
By Nature's first great title – mind!
Croly

Mountain Ash – **INTELLECT**

SEPTEMBER 5

AMARYLLIS I did woo,
And I courted Phyllis too!
Daphne for her love I chose,
Chloris for that damask rose
In her cheek, I held so dear –
Yea, a thousand like, well near,
And, in love with all together,
Feared the enjoying either;
'Cause, to be of one possess'd,
Barr'd the hope of all the rest.
Wither

Aster – **VARIETY**

SEPTEMBER 6

AND he gave the monks his treasures,
   Gave them all, with this behest:
They should feed the birds at noontide
   Daily on his place of rest.

Saying, 'From these wandering minstrels
   I have learned the art of song;
Let me now repay the lessons
   They have taught so well and long.'

Thus the Bard of Love departed;
   And, fulfilling his desire,
On his tomb the birds were feasted
   By the children of the choir.
Longfellow

Berry Wreath – **REWARD**

September 7

WITH her book, and her voice, and her lyre,
　To wing all her moments at home;
And with scenes that new rapture inspire,
　As oft as it suits her to roam;
She will have just the life she prefers,
　With little to hope or to fear;
And ours would be pleasant as hers,
　Might we view her enjoying it here.
Cowper

Nut Tree – **AMUSEMENT**

September 8

THERE is a joy, when hearts that beat together
Sit under blossoming trees, when spring is new;
There is a joy in summer's sultry weather,
When leafy boughs bend over lovers true.
There is a joy, deep in the autumn heather
To crouch with one who's all the world to you;
And joy there is, 'mid winter nights and storms,
When gleams the firelight on two happy forms.
Austin

Nutmeg Geranium – **AN EXPECTED MEETING**

September 9

OFT when, oppress'd with sad foreboding gloom,
I sat reclined upon our favourite tomb,
I've seen those sympathetic eyes o'erflow
With kind compassion for thy comrade's woe;
Or, when less mournful subjects form'd our
　　themes,
We tried a thousand fond romantic schemes;
Oft hast thou sworn, in friendship's soothing
　　tone,
Whatever wish was mine, must be thine own.
Byron

Double Aster – **RECIPROCITY**

SEPTEMBER 10

I PLEDGE you in this cup of grief,
Where floats the fennel's bitter leaf!
The battle of our life is brief:
The alarm – the struggle – the relief –
Then sleep we side by side.

Longfellow

Balm of Gilead – **RELIEF**

SEPTEMBER 11

WHEN the bright stars came out last night,
And the dew lay on the flowers,
I had a vision of delight,
A dream of bygone hours:

Those hours that came and fled so fast,
Of pleasure or of pain,
As phantoms rose from out the past
Before my eyes again.

With beating heart did I behold
A train of joyous hours,
Lit with the radiant light of old,
And smiling crown'd with flowers.

Adelaide Procter

Silver-leaved Geranium – **RETROSPECTION**

SEPTEMBER 12

GIVE me your hand: here let me kneel:
Make your reproaches sharp as steel;
Spurn me, and smite me on each cheek –
No violence can harm the meek.

Longfellow

Birch Tree – **MEEKNESS**

September 13

I RISE from dreams of thee,
   In the first sweet sleep of night,
When the winds are breathing low,
   And the stars are shining bright:

I rise from dreams of thee;
   And a spirit in my feet
Has led me – who knows how? –
   To thy chamber window, sweet!
Shelley

Dew Plant – **A Serenade**

September 14

SHE gazed upon a world she scarcely knew,
   As seeking not to know it; silent, lone,
As grows a flower, thus quietly she grew,
   And kept her heart serene within its zone.
There was awe in the homage which she drew;
Her spirit seem'd as seated on a throne,
Apart from the surrounding world, and strong
In its own strength – most strange in one so
    young.

Byron

Dahlia – **Elegance and Dignity**

September 15

'FAIN would I climb, but that I fear to fall.' –
'If thy heart fail thee, climb not at all.'
Sir Walter Raleigh and Queen Elizabeth

Single Aster – **Indecision**

SEPTEMBER 16

THEN first were diamonds from the night
Of earth's deep centre brought to light
And made to grace the conquering way
Of proud young Beauty with their ray.
Then, too, the pearl from out the shell,
Unsightly in the sunless sea
(As 'twere a spirit forced to dwell
In form unlovely), was set free,
And round the neck of woman threw
A light it lent, and borrow'd too.

Moore

Daphne – **ORNAMENT**

SEPTEMBER 17

. . . IT is in vain,
I see, to argue against the grain:
Or, like the stars, incline men to
What they're averse themselves to do;
For when disputes are wearied out,
'Tis interest still resolves the doubt:
A man convinced against his will,
Is of the same opinion still.

Butler

Fig – **ARGUMENT**

SEPTEMBER 18

LET'S take this world as some wide scene,
    Through which, in frail but buoyant boat,
With skies now dark, and now serene,
    Together thou and I must float.

Should chilling winds and rains come on,
    We'll raise our awning 'gainst the shower,
Sit closer till the storm is gone,
    And smiling wait a sunnier hour.

And if that sunnier hour should shine,
    We'll know its brightness cannot stay;
But, happy while 'tis mine and thine,
    Complain not when it fades away.

Moore

Chrysanthemum – **CHEERFULNESS**

SEPTEMBER 19

AROUND each pure domestic shrine
Bright flowers of Eden bloom and twine,
   Our hearths are alters all;
The prayers of hungry souls and poor,
Like armèd angels at the door,
   Our unseen foes appal.

Keble

Flax – **DOMESTIC VIRTUES**

SEPTEMBER 20

SUCH ones ill judge of love, that cannot love,
Ne in their frozen hearts feele kindly flame;
Forthy they ought not thing unknowne reprove.
Ne naturall affection faultless blame,
For fault of few that have abused the same;
For it of honour and all vertue is
The roote, and brings forth glorious flowres of
    fame,
That crowne true lovers with immortall bliss,
The meed of them that love, and do not love
    amisse.

Spenser

Hop – **INJUSTICE**

SEPTEMBER 21

WHAT, then, is taste, but these internal powers,
Active and strong, and feelingly alive
To each fine impulse? – a discerning sense
Of decent and sublime, with quick disgust
From things deformed, or disarranged, or gross
In species? This no gems or stores of gold,
Nor purple state, nor culture can bestow,
But God alone, when first His active hand
Imprints the secret bias of the soul.

Akenside

Fuchsia – **TASTE**

SEPTEMBER 22

WHEN any, favour'd of high Jove,
Chance to pass through this advent'rous glade,
Swift as the sparkle of a glancing star,
I shoot from heaven, to give him safe convoy.

Milton

Juniper – **PROTECTION**

SEPTEMBER 23

. . . . AND here let those
Who boast in mortal things, and wondering tell
Of Babel and the works of Memphian kings,
Learn how their greatest monuments of fame,
And strength, and art, are easily outdone
By spirits reprobate; and in an hour,
What in an age they, with incessant toil
And hands innumerable, scarce perform.

Milton

Hydrangea – **BOASTFULNESS**

SEPTEMBER 24

'TO–MORROW your Dictator
    Shall bring in triumph home
The spoils of thirty cities,
    To deck the shrines of Rome!'
Then burst from that great concourse
    A shout that shook the towers;
And some ran north, and some ran south,
    Crying, 'The day is ours!'

Macaulay

Indian Corn – **ECLAT, OR TRIUMPH**

SEPTEMBER 25

So, you think you love me, do you?
　Well, it may be so;
But there are many ways of loving,
　I have learnt to know:
Many ways, and but one true way,
　Which is very rare;
And the counterfeits look brightest,
　Though they will not wear.
Adelaide Procter

Lavender – **DISTRUST**

SEPTEMBER 26

SACRED I'll hold the sacred name of wife,
And love thee to the sunset verge of life;
Yea, shall so much of empire o'er man's soul
Live in a wanton's smile, and no control
Bind down his heart to keep a steadier faith
For links that are to last from life to death?
Let those who can in transient loves rejoice –
Still to new hopes breathe forth successive sighs;
Give me the music of the accustom'd voice,
And the sweet light of long familiar eyes.
Hon Mrs Norton

Linden – **CONJUGAL LOVE**

SEPTEMBER 27

FAIR Hope is dead, and light
　Is quench'd in night.
What sound can break the silence of despair?
　O doubting heart!
　Thy sky is overcast,
　Yet stars shall rise at last,
　Brighter for darkness past,
And angels' silver voices stir the air.
Adelaide Procter

Love-Lies-Bleeding – **HOPELESS**

SEPTEMBER 28

EARTH'S increase and foison, plenty,
Barns and garners never empty;
Vines with clust'ring bunches growing,
Plants with goodly burden bowing;
Spring come to you at the farthest,
In the very end of harvest;
Scarcity and want shall shun you,
Ceres' blessing so is on you.

Shakespeare

Maize – **PLENTY**

SEPTEMBER 29

'BELOVED Ruth!' – no more he said;
The wakeful Ruth at midnight shed
   A solitary tear:
She thought again – and did agree
With him to sail across the sea,
   And drive the flying deer.

Wordsworth

Michaelmas Daisy – **AFTERTHOUGHT**

SEPTEMBER 30

O, YOU who have the charge of Love,
   Keep him in rosy bondage bound,
As, in the fields of bliss above,
   He sits, with flow'rets fetter'd round;
Loose not a tie that round him clings,
Nor ever let him use his wings;
For ev'n an hour, a minute's flight,
Will rob the plumes of half their light;
Like that celestial bird, whose nest
   Is found beneath far Eastern skies,
Whose wings, though radiant when at rest,
   Lose all their glory when he flies.

Moore

Walnut – **STRATAGEM**

OCTOBER

Hedge parsley

Annual meadow grass

Tortoiseshell

Hawthorn

Michaelmas
daisy

Rose hips

Bleeding mycena

OCTOBER 1

To gild refinèd gold, to paint the lily,
To throw a perfume on the violet;
To smooth the ice, or add another hue
Unto the rainbow, or with taper light
To seek the beauteous eye of Heaven to garnish, –
Is wasteful and ridiculous excess.

Shakespeare

Pineapple – **PERFECTION**

OCTOBER 2

.... THE slightest feeling, stirr'd
By trivial fancy, seek
Expression in that golden word,
They tarnish while they speak.

Nay, let the heart's slow, rare decree
That word in reverence keep;
Silence herself should only be
More sacred and more deep.

Adelaide Procter

Red Chrysanthemum – **LOVE**

OCTOBER 3

WHAT is Genius? 'tis a flame
Kindling all the human frame;
'Tis a ray that lights the eye,
Soft in love, in battle high:
'Tis the lightning of the mind,
Unsubdued and undefined;
'Tis the flood that pours along
The full, clear melody of song;
'Tis the sacred boon of Heaven,
To its choicest favourites given.
They who feel, can paint it well!
What is Genius? – Byron, tell!

Percival

Plane Tree – **GENIUS**

OCTOBER 4

. . . . HIS present mind
Was under fascination; he beheld
A vision, and adored the thing he saw.
Arabian fiction never fill'd the world
With half the wonders that were wrought for him.
Earth breathed in one great presence of the Spring;
Life turned the meanest of her implements,
Before his eyes, to price above all gold.
The house she dwelt in was a sainted shrine,
Her chamber window did surpass in glory
The portals of the dawn; all Paradise
Could, by the simple opening of a door,
Let itself in upon him.

Wordsworth

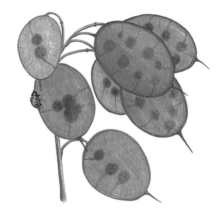

Honesty – **FASCINATION**

OCTOBER 5

TREASURE Love, though ready
   Still to live without;
In your fondest trust, keep
   Just *one* thread of doubt.

Build on no to-morrow,
   Love has but to-day;
If the links seem slackening,
   Cut the bond away.

Trust no prayer or promise;
   Words are grains of sand;
To keep your heart unbroken,
   Hold it in your hand.

Adelaide Procter

Pomegranate Blossom – **A WARNING**

OCTOBER 6

NOR was it long ere by her side
I found myself whole happy days.

Though gross the air on earth I drew,
'Twas blessèd while she breathed it too:
Though dark the flowers, though dim the sky,
Love lent them light while she was nigh.
Throughout creation, I but knew
Two separate worlds, – the *one*, that small
   Beloved and consecrated spot,
Where Lea *was*; the *other*, all
   The dull, wide waste, where she was *not*.

Moore

Azalea – **ADORATION**

OCTOBER 7

Love, that of every woman's heart
Will have the whole, and not a part;
That is to her, in Nature's plan,
More than ambition to a man, –
Her light, her life, her very breath,
With no alternative but death!
Longfellow

Hollyhock – **Female Ambition**

OCTOBER 8

Clamour grew dumb, unheard was shepherd's song,
And silence girt the woods; no warbling tongue
Talk'd to the echo; satyrs broke their dance,
And all the upper world lay in a trance.
Only the curled streams soft chidings kept;
And little gales, that from the green leaf swept
Dry summer's dust, in fearful whisperings stirr'd,
As loth to waken any singing bird.
Browne

Belladonna – **Silence**

OCTOBER 9

(To the Evening Star.)
O, sacred to the fall of day,
   Queen of propitious stars, appear!
And early rise, and long delay,
   When Caroline herself is here!

Thus, ever thus, at day's decline,
   In converse sweet, to wander far;
O, bring with thee my Caroline,
   And thou shalt be my ruling star!
Campbell

Myrtle – **Love**

OCTOBER 10

FEAR to do base, unworthy things, is valour;
If they be done to us, to suffer them,
Is valour too.

Ben Jonson

Oak Leaf – **VALOUR**

OCTOBER 11

BUT where to find that happiest spot below,
Who can direct, when all pretend to know?
The shuddering tenant of the frigid zone
Boldly proclaims the happiest spot his own,
Extols the treasures of his stormy seas,
And his long nights of revelry and ease:
The naked negro, panting at the line,
Boasts of his golden sands and palmy wine,
Basks in the glare, or stems the tepid wave,
And thanks his gods for all the good they gave.
Such is the patriot's boast; where'er we roam,
His first, best country ever is at home.

Goldsmith

Nasturtium – **PATRIOTISM**

OCTOBER 12

UPON my heart thy accents sweet,
    Of peace and pity, fell like dew
On flowers half dead; thy lips did meet
    Mine tremblingly; thy dark eyes threw
Their soft persuasion on my brain,
Charming away its dream of pain.

Shelley

Black Pine – **PITY**

OCTOBER 13

THY spirit, Independence, let me share,
  Lord of the lion heart and eagle eye!
Thy steps I follow, with my bosom bare,
  Nor heed the storm that howls along the sky.
                                                Smollett

Wild Plum Tree – **INDEPENDENCE**

OCTOBER 14

THE soul's dark cottage, battered and decayed,
Lets in new light through chinks that time has
        made;
Stronger by weakness, wiser, men become,
As they draw near to their eternal home:
Leaving the old, both worlds at once they view,
That stand upon the threshold of the new.
                                                Waller

Berberis – **AGE**

OCTOBER 15

OH! Nanny, wilt thou go with me,
  Nor sigh to leave the flaunting town?
Can silent glens have charms for thee,
  The lowly cot, and russet gown?
No longer drest in silken sheen,
  No longer deck'd with jewels rare, –
Say, canst thou quit each courtly scene,
  Where thou wert fairest of the fair?
                                                Percy

Everlasting Pea – **'WILT THOU GO WITH ME?'**

October 16

Hark! where the martial trumpet fills the air;
How the roused multitude come round to stare!
Sport drops his ball, Toil throws his hammer by,
Thrift breaks a bargain off to please his eye.
Up fly the windows; ev'n fair Mistress Cook,
Though dinner burn, must run to take a look.

Sprague

Sycamore – **Curiosity**

October 17

We need not bid, for cloister'd cell,
Our neighbour and our work farewell,
Nor strive to wind ourselves too high
For sinful man beneath the sky.

The trivial round, the common task,
Would furnish all we ought to ask:
Room to deny ourselves – a road
To bring us daily nearer God.

Keble

Thistle – **Austerity**

October 18

Oh! blest with temper, whose unchanging ray
Can make to-morrow cheerful as to-day;
She who can love a sister's charms, and hear
Sighs for a daughter with unwounded ear;
She who ne'er answers till her husband cools,
And if she rules him, never shows she rules;
Charms by accepting, by submitting, sways,
And has her humour most, when she obeys.

Pope

Valerian – **Accommodating Disposition**

October 19

IN vain all the knights of the Underwald woo'd her;
Though brightest of maidens, the proudest was she:
Brave chieftains they sought her, and young
    minstrels they sued her;
But worthy were none of the high-born ladye.

Moore

Tall Sunflower – **HAUGHTINESS**

October 20

THE mask is off – the charm is wrought –
And Selim to his heart has caught,
In blushes more than ever bright,
His Nourmahal, his Haram's Light.
And well do vanish'd frowns enhance
The charm of every brighten'd glance;
And dearer seems each dawning smile,
For having lost its light awhile:
And happier now for all her sighs,
    As on his arm her head reposes,
She whispers him, with laughing eyes,
    'Remember, love, the Feast of Roses!'

Moore

Hazel Nuts – **RECONCILIATION**

October 21

DRINK to me only with thine eyes,
    And I will pledge with mine;
Or leave a kiss within the cup,
    And I'll not ask for wine.
The thirst that from the soul doth rise,
    Doth ask a drink divine:
But, might I of Love's nectar sip,
    I would not change for thine.

Ben Jonson

Vine – **INTOXICATION**

October 22

THE foam-fringe at their feet was not more white
Than her pale cheeks, as downcast, she replied:
'No, Godfrid, no! Farewell – farewell!
   You might
Have been my star: a star fell once by pride.
But since you furl your wings and veil your light,
I cling to Mary, and Christ crucified!
Leave me – nay, leave me, ere it be too late;
Better part here, than part at heaven's gate!'
Alfred Austin

Eucalyptus – **FAREWELL**

October 23

PERSEVERANCE is a virtue
That wins each god-like act, and plucks success
E'en from the spear-proof crest of rugged
    danger.
William Havard

Canary Grass – **PERSEVERANCE**

October 24

BEFORE thy mystic altar, heavenly Truth,
I kneel in manhood, as I knelt in youth:
Thus let me kneel, till this dull form decay
And life's last shade be brighten'd by thy ray:
Then shall my soul, now lost in clouds below,
Soar without bound, without consuming glow.
Sir William Jones

White Chrysanthemum – **TRUTH**

October 25

ALL my error, all my weakness,
   All my vain delusions fled;
Hope again revived, and gladness
   Waved its wings above my head.

Like the wanderer of the desert,
   When across the weary sand
Breathes the perfume from the thickets
   Bordering on the promised land.
Aytoun

Sweet Cicely – **GLADNESS**

October 26

OLD friends, old scenes, will lovelier be,
As more of Heaven in each we see;
Some softening gleam of love and prayer
Shall dawn on every cross and care.

As for some dear familiar strain
Untired we ask, and ask again,
Ever, in its melodious store,
Finding a spell unheard before; –

Such is the bliss of souls serene,
When they have sworn, and steadfast mean,
Counting the cost, in all t'espy
Their God, in all themselves deny.
Keble

Wild Geranium – **STEADFAST PIETY**

October 27

SANGUINE he was, and studied pleasure most;
His morning's draught, sack, with a nut-brown toast.
All delicates that money could procure
He had – a nice, luxurious epicure.
Pope's 'Chaucer'

Chestnut – **LUXURY**

October 28

LET come what will, I mean to bear it out,
And either live with glorious Victory,
Or die with Fame, renown'd in chivalry.
He is not worthy of the honeycomb,
That shuns the hive because the bees have stings.
Shakespeare

Purple Columbine – **RESOLUTION**

October 29

WAIT; yet I do not tell you
　　The hour you long for now
Will not come with its radiance vanish'd
　　And a shadow upon its brow.

Yet far through the misty future,
　　With a crown of starry light,
An hour of joy you know not,
　　Is winging her silent flight.
Adelaide Procter

Dock – **PATIENCE**

October 30

Go when the morning shineth,
　　Go when the moon is bright,
Go when the eve declineth,
　　Go in the hush of night;
Go with pure mind and feeling,
　　Fling every fear away,
And in thy chamber kneeling,
　　Do thou in secret pray.
Bell

Night-scented Stock – **DEVOTION**

October 31

WHEN I sang of Ariadne,
  Sang the old and mournful tale,
How her faithless lover, Theseus,
  Left her to lament and wail; –

Then thy eyes would fill and glisten,
  Her complaint could soften thee;
Thou has wept for Ariadne –
  Theusus' self might weep for me!
Aytoun

Yellow Chrysanthemum – **SLIGHTED LOVE**

NOVEMBER

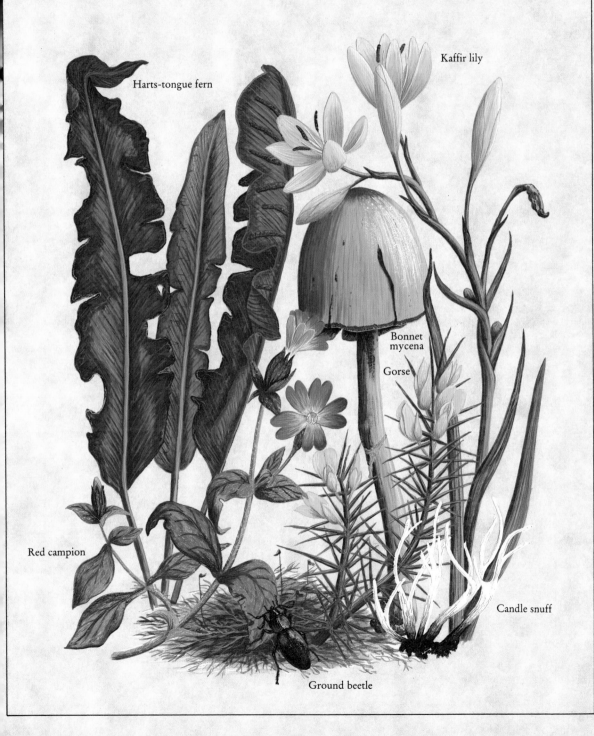

Harts-tongue fern

Kaffir lily

Bonnet mycena

Gorse

Red campion

Candle snuff

Ground beetle

November 1

The fine and noble way to kill a foe,
  Is not to kill him; you with kindness may
So change him, that he shall cease to be so,
  And then he's slain: Sigismund used to say,
His pardons put his foes to death; for when
He mortified their hate, he kill'd them then.

Aleyn

Winter Heliotrope – **Kindness**

November 2

But, O, the heavy change now thou art gone! –
Now thou art gone, and never must return!
Thee, Shepherd, thee, the woods and desert caves,
With wild thyme and the gadding vine o'ergrown,
And all their echoes mourn;
The willows, and the hazel copses green,
Shall now no more be seen
Fanning their joyous leaves to thy soft lays.
As killing as the canker to the rose,
Or taint-worm to the weanling herds that graze,
Or frost to flowers that their gay wardrobe wear,
When first the white-thorn blows:
Such, Lycidas, thy loss to shepherd's ear.

Milton

Aspen – **Lamentation**

November 3

How charming is divine Philosophy!
Not harsh and crabbed, as dull fools suppose,
But musical as is Apollo's lute,
And a perpetual feast of nectar'd sweets,
Where no crude surfeit reigns.

Milton

Pitch Pine – **Philosophy**

November 4

I KNOW where the winged visions dwell,
   That around the night-bed play;
I know each herb and flow'rets bell,
   Where they hide their wings by day.

The dream of the injured, patient mind,
   That smiles with the wrongs of men,
Is found in the bruised and wounded rind
   Of the cinnamon, sweetest then.
   Then hasten we, maid,
   To twine our braid:
To-morrow the dreams and flow'rs will fade.
Moore

Cranberry – **CURE FOR HEARTACHE**

November 5

FULL half an hour to-day I tried my lot,
   With various flowers, and every one still said,
'She loves me' – 'Loves me not!'
And if this meant a vision long since fled –
If it meant fortune, fame, or peace of thought –
If it meant – but I dread
To speak what you may know so well:
Still there was truth in that sad oracle.
Shelley

Hemp – **FATE**

November 6

IT will live, no eyes will see it;
   In my soul it will lie deep,
Hidden from all; but I shall feel it
   Often stirring in my sleep.

So remember, that the friendship
   Which you now think poor and vain,
Will endure in hope and patience,
   Till you ask for it again.
Adelaide Procter

Globe Amaranth – **UNCHANGEABLE**

November 7

BUT let my feet never fail
To walk the studious cloister's pale,
And love the high embowed roof,
With antic pillars massy proof,
And storied windows richly dight,
Casting a dim religious light.
There let the pealing organ blow,
To the full-voiced quire below,
In service high, and anthem clear,
As may with sweetness, through mine ear,
Dissolve me into ecstacies,
And bring all heaven before my eyes.
Milton

Snow Berry – **THOUGHTS OF HEAVEN**

November 8

SPIRIT, who sweepest the wild harp of Time!
It is most hard, with an untroubled ear,
Thy dark inwoven harmonies to hear!
Yet, mine eye fix'd on heaven's unchanging clime,
Long when I listen'd, free from mortal fear,
With inward stillness, and submitted mind:
When, lo! its folds far waving on the wind,
I saw the train of the departing year!
   Starting from my silent sadness,
   Then, with no unholy madness,
Ere yet the entered cloud foreclosed my sight,
I raised the impetuous song, and solemnised his flight!
Coleridge

White Poplar – **TIME**

November 9

. . . May he live
Longer than I have time to tell his years!
Ever beloved, and loving may his rule be;
And, when old Time shall lead him to his end,
Goodness and he fill up one monument.
Shakespeare

Ash Tree – **GRANDEUR**

November 10

PERHAPS in some long twilight hour,
  Like those we have known of old,
When past shadows gather round you,
  And your present friends grow cold;

You may stretch your hands out towards me, –
  Ah! you will – I know not when –
I shall nurse my love, and keep it
  Faithfully for you till then.

Adelaide Procter

Bay Leaf – **FAITHFULNESS**

November 11

EYES, eyes, that were so lovely shall I see your glance no more?
Heart, heart, that so tender, will your grief for me be sore? –
And none be near to warn thee, when he breathes his treacherous
      vow,
That he slew thine own true lover, who vainly calls thee now,
And murmurs, 'Helen! Helen!' with the death damp on his brow!
For my friend gave me false counsel, that I might die, and he might
      live;
For dear, dear, dear's the love that Helen Douglas has to give.

Hon Mrs Norton

Bilberry – **TREACHERY**

November 12

HEAVEN hath its crown of stars, the earth
  Her glory robe of flowers, –
The sea its gems, the grand old woods
  Their songs and greening showers:
The birds have homes, where leaves and blooms
  In beauty wreathe above;
High yearning hearts their rainbow dreams,
  And we, sweet – we have love!

Massey

Bindweed – **PROFUSENESS**

November 13

SHALL I be left forgotten in the dust,
    When the Fate, relenting, lets the flower revive?
Shall Nature's voice, to man alone unjust,
    Bid him, though doom'd to perish, hope to live?
Is it for this fair Virtue oft must strive
    With disappointment, penury, and pain?
No: Heaven's immortal spring shall yet arrive,
    And man's majestic beauty bloom again,
Bright through the eternal year of Love's triumphant
        reign.

Beattie

Cedar of Lebanon – **INCORRUPTIBILITY**

November 14

A VIOLET by a mossy stone,
    Half hidden from the eye, –
Fair as a star, when only one
    Is shining in the sky:

She lived unknown, and few could know
    When Lucy ceased to be;
But she is in her grave, and, oh!
    The difference to me!

Wordsworth

Bramble – **LOWLINESS**

November 15

GOLDEN sparkles, flashing gem,
Lift the robes of each of them;
Cloak of velvet, robe of silk,
Mantle snowy-white as milk;
Ring upon our bridle hand,
Jewels on our belt and band;
Bells upon our golden reins,
Tinlking spurs, and shining chains, –
In such merry mob we went,
Riding to the tournament.

Thornbury

Red Salvia – **POMP**

November 16

OH! the light of life that sparkled
  In those bright and bounteous eyes!
Oh! the blush of happy beauty,
  Tell-tale of the heart's surprise!
Oh! the radiant light that girdled
  Field and forest, land and sea,
When we all were young together,
  And the earth was new to me.

Aytoun

Variegated Ivy – **BRIGHTNESS**

November 17

YET whenever I cross the river,
  On its bridge with wooden piers,
Like the odour of brine from the ocean,
  Comes the thought of other years.

And for ever, and for ever,
  As long as the river flows, –
As long as the heart has passions,
  As long as life has woes; –

The moon and its broken reflection,
  And its shadows shall appear,
As the symbol of Love in heaven,
  And its wavering image here.

Longfellow

Hogweed – **REMEMBRANCE**

November 18

DIVINE Content!
O! could the world resent,
How much of bliss doth lie
Wrapp'd up in thy
Delicious name; and at
How low a rate
Thou might'st be bought!
No trade would driven be,
To purchase any wealth, but only thee.

Beaumont

Fern Moss – **CONTENT**

November 19

How canst thou dream of Beauty as a thing
On which depends the heart's own withering?
Lips budding red, with tints of vernal years,
And delicate lids of eyes that shed no tears,
And light that falls upon the shining hair,
As though it found a secret sunbeam there, –
These must go by, my Gertrude, must go by;
The leaf must wither, and the flower must die;
The rose can only have a rose's bloom:
Age would have wrought thy wondrous beauty's
    doom.

Hon Mrs Norton

Shasta Daisy – **Beauty**

November 20

But where is Harold? Shall I then forget
To urge the gloomy wanderer o'er the wave?
Little reck'd he of all that men regret;
No loved one now in feign'd lament could rave;
No friend the parting hand extended gave,
Ere the cold stranger pass'd to other climes;
Hard in his heart, whom charms may not enslave;
But Harold felt not as in other times,
And left without a sigh the land of war and crimes.

Byron

Acer – '**You are hard**'

November 21

Methinks I see thee stand, with pallid cheeks,
By Fra Hilario in his diocese;
As up the convent walls, in golden streaks
The ascending sunbeams mark the day's decrease;
And as he asks what there the stranger seeks,
Thy voice along the cloister whispers – Peace!

Longfellow

Gardinea – **Peace**

November 22

Oh! ever thus, from childhood's hour,
   I've seen my fondest hopes decay;
I never loved a tree or flower,
   But 'twas the first to fade away.

I never nurst a dear gazelle,
   To glad me with its soft brown eye,
But when it came to know me well,
   And love me, it was sure to die.
Moore

Black Prince Geranium – **Delusive Hopes**

November 23

Ah, God! my child! my first, my living child!
I have been dreaming of a thing like thee,
Ere since, a babe, upon the mountains wild,
I nursed my mimic babe upon my knee,
In girlhood I had visions of thee; Love
Came to my riper youth, and still I clove
Unto thine image, born within my brain,
So like, as even there thy gem had lain!
My blood! my voice! my thought! my dream
   achieved!
Oh! till this double life, I had not lived!
Wade

Sorrel – **Parental Affection**

November 24

Dim as the borrow'd beams of moon and stars,
To lone, weary, wandering travellers,
Is Reason to the soul; and as on high
Those rolling fires discover but the sky,
Not light us here, so Reason's glimmering ray
Was lent, not to assume our doubtful way,
But guide us upward to a better day.
And as those nightly tapers disappear,
When day's bright lord ascends our hemisphere;
So pale grows Reason at Religion's sight,
So dies, and so dissolves, in supernatural light.
Dryden

Tufted Vetch – **Reason**

November 25

THERE is no dearth of kindness
  In this world of ours,
Only in our blindness
  We gather thorns for flowers!

Outward we are spurning,
  Trampling one another,
While we are inly yearning
  At the name of brother.
Massey

Norway Spruce – **KINDNESS**

November 26

ARE there not aspirations in each heart,
  After a better, brighter world than this?
Longings for beings nobler in each part,
  Things more exalted, steep'd in deeper bliss?
Who gave us these? what are they? Soul, in thee
The bud is budding now for Immortality!
Nicoll

Pine Branch – **ASPIRATION**

November 27

THE might of one fair face sublimes my love,
For it hath wean'd my heart from low desires;
Nor death I heed, nor purgatory fires;
Thy beauty, antepast of joys above,
Instructs me in the bliss that saints approve:
For, oh! how good, how beautiful must be
The God that made so good a thing as thee,
So fair an image of the Heavenly Dove!
Michael Angelo

Variegated Geranium – **CHARMS OF WOMEN**

NOVEMBER 28

How lovely in her tears!
What beams her beauty darts through clouds of woe!
So Venus look'd, when, wet with silver drops,
Above the floods she raised her shining head,
Gilded the waves, and charm'd the wondering gods.

Owen

Helenium – **TEARS**

NOVEMBER 29

AND never brooch the folds combined,
Above a heart more good and kind:
Her kindness and her worth to spy,
You need but gaze on Ellen's eye.
Not Katrine, in her mirror blue,
Gives back the shaggy banks more true,
Than every free-born glance confess'd
The guileless movements of her breast.

Scott

Czar Violet – **KINDNESS AND WORTH**

NOVEMBER 30

AND dost thou ask what secret woe
　　I bear, corroding joy and youth?
And wilt thou vainly seek to know
　　A pang, ev'n thou must fail to soothe?

It is not love, it is not hate,
　　Nor low Ambition's honours lost,
That bids me loathe my present state,
　　And fly from all I prized the most.

It is that weariness that springs
　　From all I meet, or hear, or see;
To me no pleasure beauty brings,
　　Thine eyes have scarce a charm for me.

Byron

Welted Thistle – **MISANTHROPY**

DECEMBER

Winter heliotrope

Mistletoe

Polypody fern

Bjerkadera
(fungus)

Ivy

Holly

December 1

THERE be none of Beauty's daughters
    With a magic like thee;
And like music on the waters
    Is thy sweet voice to me:
When, as if its sound were causing
The charmèd ocean's pausing,
The waves lie still and gleaming,
And the lull'd winds seem dreaming,
And the midnight moon is weaving
    Her bright chain o'er the deep,
Whose breast is gently heaving,
    As an infant's asleep:
So the spirit bows before thee,
To listen and adore thee,
With a full but soft emotion,
Like the swell of summer's ocean.
                                    Byron

Monthly Rose – **ENCHANTMENT**

December 2

I SHALL know by the gleam and glitter
    Of the golden chain you wear –
By your heart's calm strength in loving,
    Of the fire they have had to bear.

Beat on, true heart, for ever;
    Shine bright, strong golden chain,
And bless the cleansing fire,
    And the furnace of living pain.
                            Adelaide Procter

Hyssop – **PURITY**

December 3

No single virtue we could most command,
Whether the wife, the mother, or the friend:
For she was all, in that supreme degree,
That as no one prevail'd, so all was she.
The several parts lay hidden in the piece,
The occasion but exerted that or this.
A wife as tender, and as true withal,
As the first woman was, before her fall;
Made for the man, of whom she was a part,
Made to attract his eyes and keep his heart.
                                    Dryden

White Camellia – **EXCELLENCE IN WOMAN**

December 4

LEARN from your orient shell to love thy foe,
And store with pearls the hand that brings thee woe;
Free, like yon rock, from base vindictive pride,
Emblaze with gems the wrist that tears thy side.
With fruit nectareous, or balmy flower,
All Nature calls aloud, 'Shall man do less,
Than heal the smiter, and the railer bless?'

Hafiz

Scotch Thistle – **RETALIATION**

December 5

YES, the year is growing old,
    And his eye is pale and blear'd;
Death, with frosty hand and cold,
    Plucks the old man by the beard –
Sorely, Sorely!

The leaves are falling, falling,
    Solemnly and slow;
Caw, caw! the rooks are calling:
    It is a sound of woe –
    A sound of woe!

Longfellow

Withered Leaves – **MELANCHOLY**

December 6

AND when to me you first made suit,
    How fair I was, you oft would say,
And, proud of conquest, pluck'd the fruit,
    Then left the blossom to decay.

Then, Earl, why didst thou leave the beds,
    Where roses and where lilies vie,
To seek a primrose, whose pale shades
    Must sicken when those gauds are by?

Mickle

Hibiscus – **CHANGE**

DECEMBER 7

DUTY, like a strict preceptor,
　　Sometimes frowns, or seems to frown;
Choose her thistle for thy sceptre,
　　While youth's roses are thy crown.

Grasp it: if thou shrink and tremble
　　Fairest damsel of the green,
Thou wilt lack the only symbol
　　That proclaims a genuine Queen.
Wordsworth

Plantain – **OBLIGATION**

DECEMBER 8

AND dreams in their development have breath;
And tears and tortures, and the touch of joy;
They leave a weight upon our waking thoughts,
They take a weight from off our waking toils;
They do divide our being; they become
A portion of ourselves, as of our time,
And look like heralds of eternity.
They speak like spirits of the past; they speak
Like sibyls of the future; they have power,
The tyranny of pleasure and of pain.
Byron

Osmunda – **DREAMS**

DECEMBER 9

PINS she sticks into my shoulder,
　　Places needles in my chair;
And when I begin to scold her,
　　Tosses back her combèd hair,
　　With so saucy, vex'd an air,
That the pitying beholder
Cannot brook that I should scold her;
Then again she comes, and bolder,
　　Blacks again this face of mine.
Bon Gaultier

Lemon – **PIQUANCY**

DECEMBER 10

FOR we were nursed upon the salfsame hill,
Fed the same flock by fountain, shade, and rill;
Together both, ere the high lawns appear'd,
Under the opening eyelids of the morn,
We drove a-field, and both together heard
What time the gray-fly winds her sultry horn;
Batt'ning our flocks with the fresh dews of night,
Oft till the star that rose at evening, bright.
Towards heaven's descent had sloped his west'ring
    wheel.

Milton

Hibernica – **STRONG FRIENDSHIP**

....

DECEMBER 11

AND I watch'd thee ever fondly –
    Watch'd thee, dearest, from afar,
With the mute and humble homage
    Of the Indian to a star.

Aytoun

Bamboo – **HOMAGE**

....

DECEMBER 12

AND ruder words will soon rush in,
To spread the breach that words begin,
And eyes forget the gentle ray
They wore in courtship's smiling day;
And voices lose all the tone that shed
A tenderness round all they said;
Till fast declining, one by one,
The sweetnesses of love are gone…

Moore

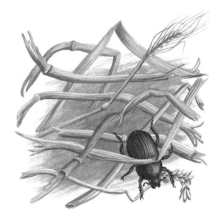

Broken Straw – **DIVISION**

....

December 13

Is thy cruse of comfort failing? – rise, and share it with
    another,
And through all the years of famine, it shall serve thee
    and thy brother.
Love Divine will fill the storehouse, and thy handful
    still renew:
Scanty fare for one, will often make a royal feast for
    two.
For the heart grows rich in giving; all its wealth is
    living gain:
Seeds, which mildew in the garner, scattered, fill with
    gold the plain.

Mrs Charles

Hips and Haws – **Compensation**

December 14

Like as the culver on the barèd bough
Sits mourning for the absence of her mate,
And in her songs sends many a wishful vow
For his return, that seems to linger late;
So I, alone now left, disconsolate,
Mourn to myself the absence of my love,
And wandering here and there, all desolate,
Seek with my plaints to match that mournful dove.

Spenser

Wormwood – **Absence**

December 15

Oh! why left I my hame?
    Why did I cross the deep?
Oh! why left I the land
    Where my forefathers sleep?
I sigh for Scotia's shore,
    And I gaze across the sea;
But I canna get a blink
    O' my ain countrie.

Gilfillan

Winter Heath – **Exile**

December 16

WHAT is earthly victory? Press on!
For it hath tempted angels – yet press on!
For it shall make you mighty among men,
And from the eyrie of your eagle thought
Ye shall look down on monarchs – O, press on!
For the high ones, and powerful, shall come
To do you reverence; and the beautiful
Will know the purer language of your brow,
And read it like a talisman of love.
Press on! for it is godlike to unloose
The spirit, and forget yourself in thought.

Willis

Douglas Fir – **PERSEVERENCE IN PURSUIT OF KNOWLEDGE**

December 17

THOUGH holy in himself, and virtuous,
He still to sinful men was mild, and piteous;
Not of reproach imperious or malign,
But in his teaching soothing and benign.
To draw them on to heaven, by reason fair
And good example, was his daily care.
But were there one perverse and obstinate,
Were he of lofty or of low estate,
Him would he sharply with reproof astound:
A better priest is nowhere to be found.
He waited not on pomp or reverence,
Nor made himself a spicèd conscience.
The love of Christ and his apostles twelve
He taught; but first he followed it himselve.

Chaucer

Flowering Laurel – **GOODNESS**

December 18

I COME – and if I come in vain,
Never, oh! never we meet again!
Thou hast done a fearful deed,
In falling away from thy fathers' creed;
But dash that turban to earth, and sign
The sign of the cross, and for ever be mine:
Wring the black drop from thy heart,
And to-morrow unites us, no more to part.

Byron

Ivy Berry – **WARNING**

DECEMBER 19

AND may at last my weary age
Find out the peaceful hermitage,
The hairy gown, and mossy cell,
Where I may sit, and rightly spell
Of every star that heaven doth show.
And every herb that sips the dew;
Till old experience do attain
To something like prophetic strain.

Milton

Moss – **SECLUSION**

DECEMBER 20

WHO seeks a friend, should come disposed
To exhibit, in full bloom disclosed,
　The graces and the beauties
That form the character he seeks;
But 'tis a union that bespeaks
　Reciprocated duties.

But will sincerity suffice?
It is indeed above all price,
　And must be made the basis;
But every virtue of the soul
Must constitute the charming whole,
　All shining in their places.

Cowper

Fern – **SINCERITY**

DECEMBER 21

ALAS! how light a cause may move
Dissension between hearts that love –
Hearts that the world in vain had tried,
And sorrow had more closely tied;
That stood the storm when waves were rough,
Yet in a sunny hour fall off;
Like ships that have gone down at sea,
When heaven was all tranquillity!
A something light as air – a look –
　A word unkind, or wrongly taken, –
Oh! love that tempests never shook,
　A breath, a touch like this, hath shaken.

Moore

Broken Stalks – **DISSENSION**

December 22

THE fire, with well-dried logs supplied,
Went roaring up the chimney wide;
The huge hall-table's oaken face,
Scrubb'd till it shone, the day to grace,
Bore then upon its massive board
No mark to part the squire and lord.
Then was brought in the lusty brawn,
By old blue-coated serving-man;
Then the grim boar's head frown'd on high,
Crested with bays and rosemary.

The wassail round, in good brown bowls
Garnish'd with ribbons, blithely trolls.
Then the huge sirloin reek'd; hard by,
Plum-porridge stood, and Christmas pie.

Scott

Parsley – FEASTING

December 23

'BUT, oh! revenge is sweet!' –
Thus think the crowd, who, eager to engage,
Take quickly fire, and kindle into rage.
Not so mild Thales nor Chrysippus thought,
Nor that good man, who drank the poisonous draught,
With mind serene, and could not wish to see
His vile accuser drink so deep as he.
Exalted Socrates! divinely brave!
Injured he fell, and dying he forgave:
Too noble for revenge, which still we find,
The weakest frailty of a feeble mind.

Dryden

Trefoil – REVENGE

December 24

AND who but listen'd, till was paid
   Respect to every inmate's claim;
The greeting given, the music played,
   In honour of each household name,
Duly pronounced, with lusty call,
And merry Christmas wish'd to all.

Wordsworth

Holly Berries – GREETINGS

December 25

But He, her fears to cease,
    Sent down the meek-eyed Peace;
She, crown'd with olive green, came softly sliding
    Down through the turning sphere,
    His ready harbinger,
With turtle wing the amorous clouds dividing;
And waving wide her myrtle wand,
She strikes an universal peace through sea and land.

    Peaceful was the night,
    Wherein the Prince of Light
His reign of peace upon the earth began:
    The winds with wonder whist,
    Smoothly the waters kist,
Whisp'ring new joys to the mild ocean,
Who now hath quite forgot to rave,
While birds of calm sit brooding on the charmed wave.

Milton

Mistletoe – '**I surmount all obstacles**'

December 26

Power laid his rod of rule aside,
And Ceremony doff'd his pride.
The heir, with roses in his shoes,
That night might village partner choose:
The lords, underogating, share
The vulgar game of 'Post and Pair.'
All hail'd, with uncontroll'd delight
And general voice, the happy night,
That to the cottage, as the crown,
Brought tidings of salvation down.

Scott

Walnuts – **Sociality**

December 27

Order is Heaven's first law – a glorious law!
Seen in those pure and beauteous isles of light,
That come and go, as circling months fulfil
Their high behest; nor less on earth discern'd
'Mid rocks snow-clad, or wastes of herbless sand;
Throughout all climes, beneath all varying skies,
Fixing for e'en the smallest flower that blooms,
Its place of growth.

Milton

Fir Cone – **Order**

DECEMBER 28

'PROPHET,' said I, 'thing of evil! – prophet still, if bird
    or devil!
By that heaven that bends above us – by that God we
    both adore –
Tell this soul with sorrow laden, if, within the distant
    Aïdenn,
It shall clasp a sainted maiden, whom the angels name
    Lenore –
Clasp a rare and radiant maiden, whom the angels
    name Lenore?'
    Quoth the Raven, 'Never more!'

Edgar Allan Poe

Holly – FORETHOUGHT

DECEMBER 29

THOUGH the doom of swift decay
    Shocks the soul, where life is strong –
Though, for frailer hearts, the day
    Lingers sad and overlong; –
Still the weight will find a leaven,
    Still the spoiler's hand is slow,
While the future has its Heaven,
    And the past, its long ago.

Lord Houghton

Helleborus – 'TRANQUILIZE MY ANXIETY'

DECEMBER 30

THEN came the merry maskers in,
And carols roar'd with blithesome din;
If unmelodious was the song,
It was a hearty note, and strong;
Who lists, might in the mumming see
Traces of ancient mystery.
White shirts supplied the masquerade,
And smutted cheeks the visors made;
But, O! what maskers richly dight
Can boast of bosoms half so light!
England was Merry England, when
Old Christmas brought his sports again.

Scott

Ash Twigs – FESTIVITY

December 31

Orphan hours, the year is dead;
   Come and sigh, come and weep!
Merry hours, smile instead,
   For the year is but asleep:
See, it smiles as it is sleeping,
Mocking your untimely weeping.

January grey is here,
   Like a sexton by her grave.
February bears the bier,
   March with grief doth howl and rave;
And April weeps – but, O ye hours!
Follow with May's fairest flowers.

Shelley

Yew – Sadness

BOTANICAL INDEX

Acacia	*Acacia pentadenia*	CHASTE LOVE	11 July
Acacia rose	*Robinia pseudocacia*	PLATONIC LOVE	29 Juiy
Acanthus	*Acanthus mollis*	THE FINE ARTS	3 May
Acer	*Acer palmatum*	'YOU ARE HARD'	20 November
Alkanet	*Anchusa officinalis*	DEVOTION	21 August
Almond tree	*Prunus dulcis*	INDISCRETION	8 February
Aloe	*Aloe aristata*	SORROW	2 September
Apple	*Malus sylvestris*	TEMPTATION	1 September
Apple blossom	*Malus sylvestris*	CHOICE	9 May
Apricot	*Prunus armeniaca*	DOUBT	13 April
Arbor vitae	*Thuja plicata*	UNCHANGING FRIENDSHIP	19 January
Arum lily	*Zantedeschia aethiopica*	ARDOUR	20 February
Ash tree	*Fraxinus excelsior*	GRANDEUR	9 November
Ash twig	*Fraxinus excelsior*	FESTIVITY	30 December
Asparagus fern	*Asparagus plumosus*	SECRECY	18 May
Aspen	*Populus tremula*	LAMENTATION	2 November
Asphodel	*Narthecium ossifragum*	'MY REGRETS FOLLOW YOU TO THE GRAVE'	15 August
Aster	*Callistephus chinensis*	VARIETY	5 September
Aster single	*Aster sativus*	INDECISION	15 September
Aster double	*Callistephus chinensis*	RECIPROCITY	9 September
Auricula	*Primula auricula*	PAINTING	17 March
Azalea	*Rhododendron javanicum*	ADORATION	6 October
Balm of Gilead	*Populus gileadensis*	RELIEF	10 September
Balsam	*Impatiens glandolifera*	IMPATIENCE	24 July
Bamboo	*Arundinaria murieliae*	HOMAGE	11 December
Banksia	*Banksia victoriae*	LOVE SWEET AND SILENT	23 August
Bay	*Laurus nobilis*	GLORY	2 January
Bay leaf	*Laurus nobilis*	FAITHFULNESS	10 November
Beech tree	*Fagus sylvatica*	PROSPERITY	5 May
Bee orchid	*Ophrys apifera*	INDUSTRY	30 July
Belladonna	*Atropa bella-donna*	SILENCE	8 October
Berberis	*Berberis darwinii*	AGE	14 October
Berry wreath	*Rubus fruiticosus, Lonicera pericylmenun, Hedera helix, Solanum dulcamara*	REWARD	6 September
Bilberry	*Vaccinium myrtillus*	TREACHERY	11 November
Bindweed	*Calystegia sepium*	PROFUSENESS	12 November
Birch	*Betula pendula*	MEEKNESS	12 September
Black pine	*Pinus nigra*	PITY	12 October
Blackthorn	*Prunus spinosa*	DIFFICULTY	8 May
Bluebell	*Endymion non-scriptus*	CONSTANCY	23 May
Borage	*Borago officinalis*	BLUNTNESS	29 August
Box	*Buxus sempervirens*	FIRMNESS	6 January
Bramble	*Rubus fruiticosus*	LOWLINESS	14 November
Broken stalks	*Silene dioica* (seed heads), *Pteriudim aquilinum*	DISSENSION	21 December
Broken straw		DIVISION	12 December
Broom	*Genista tinctoria*	HUMILITY	12 August
Bulrush	*Typha latifolia*	DOCILITY	29 February
Buttercup	*Ranunculus repens*	CHILDHOOD	28 February

Campanula	*Campanula poscharskyana*	'YOU ARE RICH IN ATTRACTION'	22 March
Camellia, white	*Camellia japonica*	EXCELLENCE IN WOMAN	3 December
Camellia, pink	*Camellia japonica*	ANTICIPATION	3 March
Camellia, red	*Camellia japonica*	PITY	6 February
Camomile	*Anthemis nobilis*	ENERGY IN ADVERSITY	30 August
Canary grass	*Phalaris arundinacea*	PERSEVERANCE	23 October
Carnation	*Dianthus*	WOMAN'S LOVE	4 July
Carnation, striped	*Dianthus*	EXTREMES	12 July
Carnation, yellow	*Dianthus*	DISDAIN	25 July
Cedar of Lebanon	*Cedrus libani*	INCORRUPTIBILITY	13 November
Celandine	*Ranunculus ficaria*	JOY	6 May
Champignon mushroom	*Agaris campestris*	SUSPICION	3 February
Cherry tree	*Prunus avium*	EDUCATION	16 April
Cherry tree, white	*Cerasus mahaleb*	DECEPTION	25 April
Chestnut	*Aesculus hippocastanum*	DO ME JUSTICE	15 May
Chestnut, horse	*Aesculus hippocastanum*	AMUSEMENT	7 September
Chestnut, Spanish	*Castanea sativa*	LUXURY	27 October
Chrysanthemum	*Chrysanthemum*	CHEERFULNESS	18 September
Chrysanthemum, red	*Chrysanthemum*	LOVE	2 October
Chrysanthemum, white	*Chrysanthemum*	TRUTH	24 October
Chrysanthemum, yellow	*Chrysanthemum*	SLIGHTED LOVE	31 October
Cineraria	*Senecio cineraria*	A STAR	25 January
Clematis	*Clematis montana*	POVERTY	4 February
Clematis	*Clematis* 'Nelly Moser'	MENTAL BEAUTY	26 August
Columbine	*Aquilegia vulgaris*	RESOLUTION	28 October
Convolvulus	*Convolvulus arvensis*	EXTINGUISHED HOPE	19 July
Corn	*Triticum*	RICHES	1 August
Cornflower	*Centaurea cyanus*	PURITY	3 August
Corsican pine	*Pinus nigra maritima*	'YOU BEWILDER ME'	1 February
Cowslip	*Primula veris*	PENSIVENESS	3 April
Cranberry	*Vaccinium oxycoccos*	CURE FOR HEARTACHE	4 November
Cress	*Lepidium sativum*	STABILITY	11 January
Crocus	*Crocus*	ABUSE NOT	5 February
Cucumber	*Cucumis sativus*	CRITICISM	12 March
Cyclamen	*Cyclamen persicum*	HOPE	25 February
Cypress	*Cupressaceae*	MOURNING	5 January
Daffodil	*Narcissus*	CHIVALRY	17 February
Daffodil, double	*Narcissus*	REGARD	13 March
Dahlia	*Dahlia*	ELEGANCE AND DIGNITY	14 September
Dahlia, red	*Dahlia* 'Arabian Night'	JOY	27 August
Daisy	*Bellis perennis*	CHEERFULNESS	18 February
Daisy, double	*Bellis* 'Goliath'	PARTICIPATION	26 March
Daisy, garden	*Bellis perennis*	'I SHARE YOUR SENTIMENTS'	27 February
Daisy, Michaelmas	*Aster novi-belgii*	AFTERTHOUGHT	29 September
Daisy, Shasta	*Chrysanthemum maximum*	BEAUTY	19 November
Daisy, wild	*Bellis perennis*	INDECISION	7 March
Daphne	*Daphne laureola*	ORNAMENT	16 September
Day lily	*Hemerocallis*	COQUETRY	15 July
Dew plant	*Drosera anglica*	A SERENADE	13 September
Dock	*Rumex obtusifolius*	PATIENCE	29 October
Douglas fir	*Pseudotsugamenziesii*	PERSEVERANCE IN PURSUIT OF KNOWLEDGE	16 December
Elder	*Sambucus nigra*	MERCY	20 May
Elm	*Ulmus procera*	DIGNITY	12 May
Endive	*Cichorium endivia*	FRUGALITY	21 January
Escallonia	*Escallona macrantha*	'I LIVE FOR THEE'	24 February
Eucalyptus	*Eucalyptus globulus*	FAREWELL	22 October
Evening primrose	*Oenothera erythrosepala*	INCONSTANCY	30 March
Everlasting pea	*Lathyrus latifolius*	'WILT THOU GO WITH ME?'	15 October
Fennel	*Foeniculum vulgare*	STRENGTH	23 January
Fern	*Asplenium scolopendrium*	SINCERITY	20 December

Fern moss	*Plagiothecium denticulatum*	CONTENT	18 November
Fig	*Figus carica*	ARGUMENT	17 September
Filbert tree	*Coryllus avellana*	RECONCILIATION	29 April
Fir	*Abies*	ELEVATION	15 January
Fir cone	*Abies*	ORDER	27 December
First rose of summer	*Rosa rugosa*, hybrid	MAJESTY	24 May
Flax	*Linum perenne*	DOMESTIC VIRTUES	19 September
Flowering currant	*Ribes*	SELF-REVERENCE	19 February
Forget-me-not	*Myosotis sylvatica*	'FORGET ME NOT'	1 May
Fuschia	*Fuschia riccartonii*	TASTE	21 September
Gardenia	*Gardenia jasminoides*	PEACE	21 November
Garden anemone	*Anemone orientalis*	FORSAKEN	5 March
Garden forget-me-not	*Myosotis arvensis*	'FORGET ME NOT'	6 April
Geranium, 'Black Prince'	*Pelargonium*	DELUSIVE HOPES	22 November
Geranium, ivy-leaved	*Pelargonium deltatum*	GENIUS	18 July
Geranium, nutmeg	*Pelargonium fragans*	AN EXPECTED MEETING	8 September
Geranium, oak-leaved	*Pelargonium quercifolium*	LADY, DEIGN TO SMILE	11 August
Geranium, pink	*Pelargonium*	PARTIALITY	8 August
Geranium, scarlet	*Pelargonium zonale*	COMFORT	13 July
Geranium, silver-leaved	*Pelargonium*	RETROSPECTION	11 September
Geranium, variegated	*Pelargonium x hortorum* 'Henry Cox'	CHARMS OF WOMEN	27 November
Geranium, white	*Pelargonium*	REFINEMENT	3 September
Geranium, wild	*Geranium robertianum*	STEADFAST PIETY	26 October
Globe amaranth	*Gomphrena globosa*	UNCHANGEABLE	6 November
Globe ranunculus	*Trollius europaeas*	'I AM DAZZLED BY YOUR CHARMS'	10 April
Gorse	*Olex europaeus*	ENDURING AFFECTION	21 February
Grass	*Holcus mollis*	UTILITY	1 January
Ground ivy	*Glechoma hederacea*	HUMILITY	24 January
Guelder rose	*Viburnum opulus*	GROWING OLD	9 July
Harebell	*Campanula rotundifolia*	GRIEF	14 May
Hawthorn	*Crataegus monogyna*	HOPE	17 May
Hazelnuts	*Corylus avellana*	RECONCILIATION	20 October
Heartsease	*Viola tricolor*	THOUGHTS	29 March
Heath	*Erica cinerea*	SOLITUDE	10 January
Helenium	*Helenium autumnale*	TEARS	28 November
Helleborus	*Helleborus viridis*	'TRANQUILIZE MY ANXIETY'	29 December
Hemp	*Sparmannia africana*	FATE	5 November
Hepatica	*Hepatica nobilis*	CONFIDENCE	26 February
Hibernica	*Hedera helix* 'Hibernica'	STRONG FRIENDSHIP	10 December
Hibiscus	*Hibiscus rosa-sinensis*	CHANGE	6 December
Hips and Haws	*Crataegus monogyna, Rosa rugosa* hybrid	COMPENSATION	13 December
Hogweed	*Heracleum sphondylium*	REMEMBRANCE	17 November
Holly	*Ilex aquifolium*	FORETHOUGHT	28 December
Holly berries	*Ilex aquifolium*	GREETING	24 December
Holly, variegated	*Ilex aquifolium* 'Aueomarginata ovata'	ALWAYS CHEERFUL	30 January
Hollyhock	*Alcea rosea*	FEMALE AMBITION	7 October
Holm oak	*Quercus ilex*	ENDURANCE	22 January
Honesty	*Lunaria annua*	FASCINATION	4 October
Honesty, flowers	*Lunaria rediviva*	IMMORTALITY	28 April
Honeysuckle	*Lonicera periclymenum*	RUSTIC BEAUTY	23 July
Honeysuckle, coral	*Lonicera periclymenum*	'THE COLOUR OF MY FATE'	16 August
Hop	*Humulus lupulus*	INJUSTICE	20 September
Houseleek	*Sempervivum*	VIVACITY	12 January
Hyacinth	*Hyancinthus orientalis*	SPORT	6 March
Hyacinth, blue	*Hyacinthus orientalis*	CONSTANCY	20 March
Hyacinth, purple	*Hyacinthus orientalis*	SORROW	2 April
Hydrangea	*Hydrangea macrophylla*	BOASTFULNESS	23 September
Hyssop	*Hyssopus officinalis*	PURITY	2 December

Ice plant	*Sedum spectabile*	REJECTED ADDRESSES	7 January
Iceland moss	*Cetraria islandica*	HEALTH	16 January
Indian corn	*Zea mays*	ECLAT, OR TRIUMPH	24 September
Indian pink	*Dianthus chinensis*	ALWAYS LOVELY	13 August
Iris	*Iris xiphioides*	I HAVE A MESSAGE FOR YOU	6 July
Ivy	*Hedera helix*	FRIENDSHIP	3 January
Ivy, berries	*Hedera helix*	WARNING	18 December
Ivy, Irish	*Hedera helix*	CLINGING AFFECTION	15 February
Ivy, spray	*Hedera helix*	ASSIDUOUS TO PLEASE	8 March
Ivy, variegated	*Hedera helix*	BRIGHTNESS	16 November
Ivy, white	*Hedera canariensis* 'Variegata'	RARITY	31 January
Japonica	*Chaenomeles japonica*	LOVE AT FIRST SIGHT	14 February
Jasmine, Madagascar	*Stephanotis floribunda*	SEPARATION	24 August
Jasmine, white	*Jasminum officinalis*	EXTREME AMIABILITY	20 July
Jasmine, yellow	*Jasminum nudiflorum*	GRACE AND ELEGANCE	10 August
Juniper	*Juniperus communis*	PROTECTION	22 September
Kalmia	*Kalmia latifolia*	NATURE	9 February
Kingcup	*Caltha palustris*	'I WISH I WAS RICH'	9 March
Knotweed	*Polygonum polystachyum*	RECANTATION	28 July
Laburnum	*Laburnum anagyroides*	FORSAKEN	22 May
Larch	*Larix decidua*	DECEITFUL CHARMS	12 February
		DARING	27 April
Larkspur	*Consolida regalis*	BRIGHTNESS	22 July
Laurel	*Aucuba japonica*	AMBITION	4 January
Laurel, flowering	*Aucuba japonica*	GOODNESS	17 December
Laurel, variegated	*Aucuba japonica variegata*	ATTRACTIVE	23 February
Lauristinus	*Viburnum tinus*	'I DIE IF NEGLECTED'	20 January
Lavender	*Lavandula officinalis*	DISTRUST	25 September
Lenten lily	*Narcissus pseudonarcissus*	RECIPROCAL LOVE	25 March
Lemon	*Citrus limonum*	PIQUANCY	9 December
Lichen	*Ramalina curnowii, Cladonia coccifera*	DEJECTION	14 January
Lilac	*Syringa vulgaris*	FIRST EMOTIONS OF LOVE	13 May
Lily of the valley	*Convallaria majalis*	RETURN OF HAPPINESS	26 May
Lily, imperial	*Fritillaria imperialis*	DIGNITY	7 July
Lily, white	*Lilium regale*	PURITY	2 July
Lily, yellow	*Lilium x aurelianense*	FALSEHOOD	21 July
Linden	*Citrus acris*	CONJUGAL LOVE	26 September
Lotus	*Nelumbo nicifera*	ELOQUENCE	16 July
Lotus flower	*Nymphaea alba*	ESTRANGED LOVE	14 July
Love-lies-bleeding	*Amaranthus caudatus*	HOPELESS	27 September
Magnolia	*Magnolia alba*	LOVE OF NATURE	17 July
Maize	*Zea mays*	PLENTY	28 September
Marjoram	*Origanum vulgare*	BLUSHES	14 April
Marshmallow	*Althaea officinalis*	KINDNESS	11 March
Meadow saffron	*Colchicum autumnale*	MIRTH	8 April
Mignonette	*Reseda odorata*	EXCELLENCE	5 July
Mint	*Mentha spicata*	VIRTUE	14 March
Mistletoe	*Viscum album*	'I SURMOUNT ALL OBSTACLES'	25 December
Monkshood	*Aconitum napellus*	FICKLENESS	17 August
Monterey cypress	*Cupressus macrocarpa*	CONSTANT	18 January
Monthly honeysuckle	*Lonicera periclymenum*	BOND OF LOVE	31 August
Monthly rosebud	'Excelsa'	ENCHANTMENT	1 December
Moss	*Fissidens bryoides*	SECLUSION	19 December
Mountain ash	*Sorbus aucuparia*	INTELLECT	4 September
Mustard	*Alliaria petiolata*	INDIFFERENCE	16 March
Myrtle	*Myrtus communis*	LOVE	9 October
Narcissus	*Narcissus*	EGOTISM	7 May
Nasturtium	*Tropagolum*	PATRIOTISM	11 October

Night-scented stock	*Mathiola bicornis*	DEVOTION	30 October
Norway spruce	*Picea abies*	KINDNESS	25 November
Oak	*Quercus cerris*	HOSPITALITY	29 May
Oak, leaves	*Quercus robur*	VALOUR	10 October
Oats	*Avena*	MUSIC	5 August
Olive	*Olea europaea*	PEACE	27 January
Opuntia	*Opuntia salmiana*	SATIRE	7 February
Orange	*Citrus vulgaris*	GENEROSITY	17 January
Orange, blossom	*Citrus aurantium*	CHASTITY	19 March
Orchis	*Pleione formosana*	A BEAUTY	23 March
Osier	*Salix viminalis*	CANDOUR	21 May
Osmundia	*Osmunda regalis*	DREAMS	8 December
Palm	*Howea forteriana*	VICTORY	1 April
Parsley	*Carum petroselinum*	FEASTING	22 December
Passion flower	*Passiflora caerulea*	BELIEF	27 July
Peach blossom	*Prunus davidiana*	'I AM YOUR CAPTIVE'	12 April
Pear tree	*Pyrus communis*	AFFECTION	7 April
Peony	*Paeonia officinalis*	ANGER	14 August
Peppermint	*Mentha piperata*	CORDIALITY	27 March
Periwinkle, blue	*Vinca major*	PLEASURES OF MEMORY	20 April
Periwinkle, red	*Vinca rosea*	EARLY FRIENDSHIPS	18 March
Periwinkle, white	*Vinca minor*	PLEASANT RECOLLECTIONS	28 March
Pimpernel	*Anagallis tenella*	CHANGE	25 May
Pineapple	*Ananas comosus*	PERFECTION	1 October
Pine branch	*Pinus*	ASPIRATION	26 November
Pink	*Dianthus*	BOLDNESS	1 July
Pink, mountain	*Dianthus*	AMBITION	31 July
Pink, red double	*Dianthus*	ARDENT LOVE	10 July
Pink, white	*Dianthus*	'YOU ARE FAIR AND FASCINATING'	26 July
Pitch pine	*Pinus rigida*	PHILOSOPHY	3 November
Plantain	*Plantago laceolate*	OBLIGATION	7 December
Plane	*Platanus hybrida*	GENIUS	3 October
Plum tree	*Prunus domesticus*	INDEPENDENCE	13 October
Polyanthus	*Primula, hybrid*	PRIDE OF RICHES	31 March
Polyanthus, crimson	*Primula vulgaris*	THE HEART'S MYSTERY	5 April
Polyanthus, lilac	*Primula, hybrid*	CONFIDENCE IN HEAVEN	9 April
Polypody fern	*Polypodium interjectum*	MEDITATION	10 May
Pomegranite	*Punica granatum*	FOLLY	28 August
Pomegranite, blossom	*Punica granatum*	A WARNING	5 October
Poplar	*Populus nigra*	COURAGE	27 May
Poplar, white	*Populus alba*	TIME	8 November
Poppy, crimson	*Papaver orientalis*	FANTASY	9 August
Poppy, field	*Papaver rhoeas*	CONSOLATION	2 August
Poppy, tree	*Romneya coulteri*	LOVE'S ORACLE	13 February
Poppy, white	*Papaver orientalis* 'Perry's White'	SLEEP	7 August
Primrose	*Primula vulgaris*	YOUTH	15 March
Primrose, red	*Primula vulgaris*	UNPATRONIZED MERIT	11 April
Primula	*Primula, hybrid*	ANIMATION	10 February
Quaking grass	*Briza media*	AGITATION	18 August
Red salvia	*Salvia splendens*	POMP	15 November
Rhubarb	*Rheum rhaponticum*	ADVICE	21 March
Rhododendron	*Rhododendron* 'Elizabeth'	DANGER	11 May
Rose, apricot	'Helen Traubel'	'WELCOME ME'	2 June
Rose, Austrian	*Rosa foetida*	'THOU ART ALL THAT IS LOVELY'	5 June
Rose, burgundy	*Hybrid tea* 'Guinee'	UNCONCIOUSNESS	6 June
Rose, boursault	*Boursault*	HAPPY LOVE	4 June
Rose, cabbage	*Rosa centifolia*	AMBASSADOR	3 June
Rose, Caroline	*Foliacée*	LOVE IS DANGEROUS	8 June
Rose, china	*Rosa chinensis*	GRACE	11 June

Rose, cluster	'Sanders' White'	'YOU ARE CHARMING'	19 June
Rose, crown of roses	Rambler, *Rugosa*	REWARD OF CHASTITY	30 June
Rose, damask	*Rosier de Damas*	FRESHNESS	25 June
Rose, deep red	*Rosa* 'Provence'	BASHFULNESS	13 June
Rose, Gloire de Dijon	*Gloire de Dijon*	GLADNESS	1 June
Rose, Holy	*Rosa x Richardii*	PRIDE	15 June
Rose, Lancaster	*Rosa gallica officinalis*	UNION	18 June
Rose, Maiden's Blush	*Rosa alba*	TIMID LOVE	28 June
Rose, moss	*Rosa centifolia muscosa*	SUPERIOR MERIT	16 June
Rose, moss rosebud	*Rosa centifolia muscosa*	CONFESSIONS OF LOVE	14 June
Rose, Mundi	*Rosa gallica versicolour*	VARIETY	26 June
Rose, musk	*Rosa brunonii*	A CAPRICIOUS BEAUTY	20 June
Rose, rambler	'Excelsa'	'ONLY DESERVE MY LOVE'	12 June
Rose, red-leaved	Hybrid tea	BEAUTY	10 June
Rose, red rosebud	*Rosa* 'Aloha'	'YOU ARE YOUNG AND BEAUTIFUL'	21 June
Rose, Unique	'Unica alba'	MODESTY	7 June
Rose, Virginian	*Rosa* 'Virginia'	COMPASSION	17 June
Rose, white	*Bourbon*	'I AM WORTHY OF YOU'	27 June
Rose, white and red	*Perle des Panachées*	UNITY	24 June
Rose, white rosebud	'Sanders' White'	A HEART IGNORANT OF LOVE	9 June
Rose, withered white	Hybrid tea	TRANSIENT IMPRESSIONS	29 June
Rose, yellow	Hybrid tea	DEPARTURE OF LOVE	22 June
Rose, York	*Rosa x alba*	WAR	23 June
Rush	*Juncus effusus*	MUSIC	22 February
Saffron	*Crocus sativus*	MARRIAGE	2 May
Sage	*Salvia officinalis*	DOMESTIC VIRTUES	13 January
Shamrock	*Oxalis acetosella*	JOY IN SORROW	23 April
Snapdragon	*Antirrhinum majus*	PRESUMPTION	19 August
Snowberry	*Symphoricarpos rivularis*	THOUGHTS OF HEAVEN	7 November
Snowdrops	*Galanthus nivalis*	HOPE	2 February
Sorrel	*Rumex acetosa*	PARENTAL AFFECTION	23 November
Southernwood	*Artemisia abrotanum*	MERRIMENT	30 May
Speedwell	*Veronica persica*	'YOU ARE MY DIVINITY'	26 April
Spring crocus	*Crocus albiflorus*	YOUTHFUL GLADNESS	11 February
Stock	*Matthiola incana*	PROMPTITUDE	20 August
Stonecrop	*Sedum anglicum*	TRANQUILLITY	28 January
Strawberry tree	*Arbutus unedo*	LOVE OR FRIENDSHIP	8 January
Sunflower	*Helianthus rigidus*	ADORATION	22 August
Sunflower, tall	*Helianthus annus*	HAUGHTINESS	19 October
Sweetbriar	*Rosa rubiginosa*	SIMPLICITY	18 April
Sweet cicely	*Myrrhis odorata*	GLADNESS	25 October
Sweet pea	*Lathryus odoratus*	DEPARTURE	3 July
Sycamore	*Acer pseudoplatanus*	CURIOSITY	16 October
Syringa	*Syringa vulgaris*	MEMORY	19 May
Tendrils of climbing plants	*Nicia sativa, Vitis vinifera*	LINKS	19 April
Thistle	*Cirsium vulgare*	AUSTERITY	17 October
Thistle, scotch	*Onopordum acanthium*	RETALIATION	4 December
Thistle, welted	*Carduus acanthoides*	MISANTHROPY	30 November
Thyme	*Thymus serpyllum*	THRIFTINESS	26 January
Traveller's joy	*Clematis vitalba*	SAFETY	4 August
Trefoil	*Lotus corniculatus*	REVENGE	23 December
Truffle	*Tuber melanospermum*	SURPRISE	29 January
Tufted vetch	*Viccia cracca*	REASON	24 November
Tulip, red	*Tulipa*	DECLARATION OF LOVE	22 April
		CONFESSIONS OF LOVE	28 May
Tulip, tree	*Liriodendron tulipifera*	FAME	31 May
Turnip	*Brassica rapa*	CHARITY	9 January
Valerian	*Centranthus ruber*	ACCOMMODATING DISPOSITION	18 October
Venus's looking glass	*Legousia hybrida*	FLATTERY	25 August
Verbena	*Verbena hybrida*	ENCHANTMENT	8 July

Vine	*Vitis vinifera*	INTOXICATION	21 October
Violet, blue	*Viola canina*	FAITHFULNESS	2 March
Violet, 'Csar'	*Viola 'Csar'*	KINDNESS AND WORTH	29 November
Violet, purple	*Viola riviniana*	'YOU OCCUPY MY THOUGHTS'	16 February
Violet, white	*Viola odorata*	MODESTY	10 March
Violet, wild	*Viola odorata*	LOVE IN IDLENESS	24 March
Virginia creeper	*Parthenocissus quinquefolia*	SWEET NEGLECT	4 May
Wallflower	*Cheiranthus cheiri*	FIDELITY	4 March
Walnuts	*Juglans regia*	SOCIALITY	26 December
Walnut tree	*Juglans regia*	STRATAGEM	30 September
Water lily	*Nymphaea*	INVOCATION	16 May
Wheat	*Triticum*	PROSPERITY	6 August
Wild ranunculus	*Ranunculus acris*	INCONSTANCY	15 April
Willow, goat	*Salix caprea*	FORSAKEN	1 March
Willow, water	*Salix viminalis*	FREEDOM	24 April
Willow, weeping	*Salix babylonica*	MELANCHOLY	30 April
Winter heath	*Erica darleyensis*	EXILE	15 December
Winter heliotrope	*Petasites fragrans*	KINDNESS	1 November
Wistaria	*Wistaria sinensis*	REGRET	17 April
Withered leaves		MELANCHOLY	5 December
Wood anemone	*Anemone nemerosa*	SICKNESS	4 April
Wood sorrel	*Oxalis acetosella*	JOY	21 April
Wormwood	*Artemisia absinthium*	ABSENCE	14 December
Yew	*Taxus baccata*	SADNESS	31 December

ACKNOWLEDGEMENTS

I am indebted to the numerous people who devoted their time and resourcefulness to collecting many of the specimens. To my wife in particular for shouldering totally the responsibilities of running and maintaining the household, thus allowing me the maximum time in which to paint. My long overdue thanks to Dagmar Thierfelder for the constant and very necessary supply of brushes and finally to Pat Howells who at the eleventh hour came to my rescue with her typewriter.